WRITING WITHOUT TEACHERS

Writing Without Teachers

PETER ELBOW

OXFORD UNIVERSITY PRESS
London   Oxford   New York

OXFORD UNIVERSITY PRESS
Oxford   London   Glasgow
New York   Toronto   Melbourne   Wellington
Nairobi   Dar es Salaam   Cape Town
Kuala Lumpur   Singapore   Jakarta   Hong Kong   Tokyo
Delhi   Bombay   Calcutta   Madras   Karachi

This book is dedicated to those people who actually use it—not just read it.

MANY people are now trying to become less helpless, both personally and politically: trying to claim more control over their own lives. One of the ways people most lack control over their own lives is through lacking control over words. Especially written words. Words come at you on a piece of paper and you often feel helpless before them. And when you want to put some words of your own back on another piece of paper, you often feel even more helpless. This book tries to show how to gain control over words, but it requires working hard and finding others to work with you. I am trying to talk to all who want to work on their writing and I feel it as a huge and diverse audience: young people and adults in school, but especially young people and adults not in school.

Most books on writing try to describe the characteristics of good writing so as to help you produce it, and the characteristics of bad writing to help you avoid it. But not this book. Here you will find no descriptions of good and bad constructions, strong and weak sentences, correct and incorrect usages. When people try to tell me about good and bad writing it doesn't usually improve my writing at all; and when I try to tell other people it seldom improves their writing either. If you want a book to tell you the characteristics of good and bad writing, this is not it.

Instead I try for two things: 1) to help you actually generate words better—more freely, lucidly, and powerfully: not make judgments about words but generate them better; 2) to help you improve your ability to make your *own* judgment about which parts of your own writing to keep and which parts to throw away.

The first three chapters help you generate words better: I give you an all-purpose writing exercise that improves the very process by which words come to you; I propose a way to make sense out of the confusing process of writing something; and I give concrete suggestions about how to have a better time writing.

The fourth and fifth chapters help you improve your own judgment about good and bad writing by helping you set up a teacherless writing class to learn how your words affect actual readers.

The appendix essay is not aimed at your writing. It represents my own desire to work out as carefully as I can—and share with those who may be curious—the premises and implications of this approach to writing better and seeking the truth about words.

The authority I call upon in writing a book about writing is my own long-standing difficulty in writing. It has always seemed to me as though people who wrote without turmoil and torture were in a completely different universe. And yet advice about writing always seemed to come from them and therefore to bear no relation to us who struggled and usually failed to write. But in the last few years I have struggled more successfully to get things written and make them work for at least some readers, and in watching myself do this I have developed the conviction I can give advice that speaks more directly to the experience of having a hard time writing. I have also reached the conviction that if you have special difficulty in writing, you are not necessarily further from writing well than someone who writes more easily.

A note to teachers. Though I particularly want this book to help students not enrolled in a writing class and people out of school altogether, nevertheless I think that most of the book will also be useful to students in a writing course. No matter what kind of writing course it might be, no matter what the age group, students will benefit from the freewriting exercises, the model of the writing process, the advice for self-management based on that model, and the techniques for finding out what words do to actual readers.

But what about the teacherless writing class itself? Can it have a teacher? Yes and no. I find I can set up a teacherless writing class in my own class *as long as I follow all the same procedures as everyone else:* I too must put in my piece of writing each week; I too must get everyone's responses and reactions to it; I too must give my own reactions to other pieces of writing. I find I'm most useful to a class if I submit pieces of writing that I'm still unsure of (which is almost unavoidable if I have to come up with something every week), and if I reveal my own reactions to other pieces of writing in such a way that students can feel these reactions are very much mine, personal, and idiosyncratic—not attempts to attain some general or correct perception of the words. When I succeed at this I help break the ice and encourage them to share their reactions and responses even if they don't trust them. In short, I can only set up something like the teacherless class in my own class if I adopt more the role of a learner and less the role of a teacher.

In proposing the teacherless writing class I am not trying to deny that there are good writing teachers. I know a few and it is impossible to miss them: they are people who simply succeed in helping most of their students write better and more satisfyingly. But they are exceedingly rare. Any such teacher should keep up whatever he or she is doing and try to tell others what it is. Any student of such a teacher should also keep it up and be grateful.

But in proposing the teacherless writing class I am trying to deny something—something that is often assumed: *the necessary connection between learning and teaching.* The teacherless writing class is a place where there is learning but no teaching. It is possible to learn something and not be taught. It is possible to be a student and not have a teacher. If the student's function is to learn and the teacher's to teach, then the student can function without a teacher, but the teacher cannot function without a student. I was surprised and chagrined that in twenty years of being a student and eight years of teaching I had not before formulated this homely truth. I think teachers learn to be more *useful* when it is clearer that they are not *necessary*. The teacherless class has helped me as a teacher because it an ideal laboratory for learning along with students and being useful to them in that way. I think it can help other teachers in the same way.

I cannot adequately thank here all the people who have helped me in writing this book. In particular there are too many people to mention who have been members of experimental teacherless writing classes who have helped me learn by letting me listen to tapes of some of their classes. And I am grateful to the students of my own classes for what I have learned. In various ways the following people have particularly helped or taught me in my efforts to write this book: Max Day, Sally Dufek, A. R. Gurney, Cris Jones, Frank Pierce Jones, Mark Levensky, Jane Martin, Phyllis Stevens, Terry Walsh, Minor White, John Wright. This book wouldn't have been possible without the example and support of Ken Macrorie. My greatest gratitude is to my wife Cami for her reactions, suggestions, proofreading, and above all for her loving support.

Olympia, Washington   P.E.
February 1973

Contents

WRITING WITHOUT TEACHERS

Freewriting Exercises

THE most effective way I know to improve your writing is to
do freewriting exercises regularly. At least three times a week.
They are sometimes called "automatic writing," "babbling,"
or "jabbering" exercises. The idea is simply to write for ten
minutes (later on, perhaps fifteen or twenty). Don't stop for
anything. Go quickly without rushing. Never stop to look
back, to cross something out, to wonder how to spell something, to wonder what word or thought to use, or to think
about what you are doing. If you can't think of a word or a
spelling, just use a squiggle or else write, "I can't think of it."
Just put down something. The easiest thing is just to put
down whatever is in your mind. If you get stuck it's fine to
write "I can't think what to say, I can't think what to say" as
many times as you want; or repeat the last word you wrote
over and over again; or anything else. The only requirement
is that you *never* stop.

What happens to a freewriting exercise is important. It
must be a piece of writing which, even if someone reads it,
doesn't send any ripples back to you. It is like writing something and putting it in a bottle in the sea. The teacherless
class helps your writing by providing maximum feedback.

Freewritings help you by providing no feedback at all. When
I assign one, I invite the writer to let me read it. But also tell
him to keep it if he prefers. I read it quickly and make no
comments at all and I do not speak with him about it. The
main thing is that a freewriting must never be evaluated in
any way; in fact there must be no discussion or comment at
all.

Here is an example of a fairly coherent exercise (sometimes
they are very incoherent, which is fine):

I think I'll write what's on my mind, but the only thing on my
mind right now is what to write for ten minutes. I've never done
this before and I'm not prepared in any way—the sky is cloudy
today, how's that? now I'm afraid I won't be able to think of what
to write when I get to the end of the sentence—well, here I am at
the end of the sentence—here I am again, again, again, again, at
least I'm still writing—Now I ask is there some reason to be happy
that I'm still writing—ah yes! Here comes the question again—
What am I getting out of this? What point is there in it? It's almost obscene to always ask it but I seem to question everything
that way and I was gonna say something else pertaining to that
but I got so busy writing down the first part that I forgot what I
was leading into. This is kind of fun oh don't stop writing—cars
and trucks speeding by somewhere out the window, pens clittering
across peoples' papers. The sky is still cloudy—is it symbolic that I
should be mentioning it? Huh? I dunno. Maybe I should try
colors, blue, red, dirty words—wait a minute—no can't do that,
orange, yellow, arm tired, green pink violet magenta lavender red
brown black green—now that I can't think of any more colors—
just about done—relief? maybe.

HOW FREEWRITING EXERCISES HELP

Freewriting may seem crazy but actually it makes simple
sense. Think of the difference between speaking and writing.
Writing has the advantage of permitting more editing. But

that's its downfall too. Almost everybody interposes a massive and complicated series of editings between the time words start to be born into consciousness and when they finally come off the end of the pencil or typewriter onto the page. This is partly because schooling makes us obsessed with the "mistakes" we make in writing. Many people are constantly thinking about spelling and grammar as they try to write. I am always thinking about the awkwardness, wordiness, and general mushiness of my natural verbal product as I try to write down words.

But it's not just "mistakes" or "bad writing" we edit as we write. We also edit unacceptable thoughts and feelings, as we do in speaking. In writing there is more time to do it so the editing is heavier: when speaking, there's someone right there waiting for a reply and he'll get bored or think we're crazy if we don't come out with *something*. Most of the time in speaking, we settle for the catch-as-catch-can way in which the words tumble out. In writing, however, there's a chance to try to get them right. But the opportunity to get them right is a terrible burden: you can work for two hours trying to get a paragraph "right" and discover it's not right at all. And then give up.

Editing, *in itself,* is not the problem. Editing is usually necessary if we want to end up with something satisfactory. The problem is that editing goes on *at the same time* as producing. The editor is, as it were, constantly looking over the shoulder of the producer and constantly fiddling with what he's doing while he's in the middle of trying to do it. No wonder the producer gets nervous, jumpy, inhibited, and finally can't be coherent. It's an unnecessary burden to try to think of words and also worry at the same time whether they're the right words.

The main thing about freewriting is that it is *nonediting*. It is an exercise in bringing together the process of producing words and putting them down on the page. Practiced regularly, it undoes the ingrained habit of editing at the same time you are trying to produce. It will make writing less blocked because words will come more easily. You will use up more paper, but chew up fewer pencils.

Next time you write, notice how often you stop yourself from writing down something you were going to write down. Or else cross it out after it's written. "Naturally," you say, "it wasn't any good." But think for a moment about the occasions when you spoke well. Seldom was it because you first got the beginning just right. Usually it was a matter of a halting or even garbled beginning, but you kept going and your speech finally became coherent and even powerful. There is a lesson here for writing: trying to get the beginning just right is a formula for failure—and probably a secret tactic to make yourself give up writing. Make some words, whatever they are, and then grab hold of that line and reel in as hard as you can. Afterwards you can throw away lousy beginnings and make new ones. This is the quickest way to get into good writing.

The habit of compulsive, premature editing doesn't just make writing hard. It also makes writing dead. Your voice is damped out by all the interruptions, changes, and hesitations between the consciousness and the page. In your natural way of producing words there is a sound, a texture, a rhythm—a voice—which is the main source of power in your writing. I don't know how it works, but this voice is the force that will make a reader listen to you, the energy that drives the meanings through his thick skull. Maybe you don't *like* your voice; maybe people have made fun of it. But it's the only voice you've got. It's your only source of power. You better get back into it, no matter what you think of it. If you keep writing in it, it may change into something you like better. But if you abandon it, you'll likely never have a voice and never be heard.

Freewritings are vacuums. Gradually you will begin to carry over into your regular writing some of the voice, force, and connectedness that creep into those vacuums.

FREEWRITING AND GARBAGE

I find freewriting offends some people. They accuse it of being an invitation to write garbage.

Yes and No.

Yes, it produces garbage, but that's all right. What is feared seems to be some kind of infection: "I've struggled so hard to make my writing cleaner, more organized, less chaotic, struggled so hard to be less helpless and confused in the face of a blank piece of paper. And I've made some progress. If I allow myself to write garbage or randomness *even for short periods,* the chaos will regain a foothold and sneak back to overwhelm me again."

Bad writing doesn't infect in this way. It might if you did nothing but freewriting—if you gave up all efforts at care, discrimination, and precision. But no one asks you to give up careful writing. It turns out, in fact, that these brief exercises in not caring help you care better afterward.

A word about being "careless." In freewriting exercises you should not stop, go back, correct, or reflect. In a sense this means "be careless." But there is a different kind of carelessness: not giving full attention, focus, or energy. Freewriting helps you pour *more* attention, focus, and energy into what you write. That is why freewriting exercises must be short.

If there is any validity to the infectious model of bad writing, it works the other way around: there is garbage in your head; if you don't let it out onto paper, it really will infect everything else up there. Garbage in your head poisons you. Garbage on paper can safely be put in the wastepaper basket.

In a sense I'm saying, "Yes, freewriting invites you to write garbage, but it's good for you." But this isn't the whole story. Freewriting isn't just therapeutic garbage. It's also a way to produce bits of writing that are genuinely *better* than usual: less random, more coherent, more highly organized. This may happen soon in your freewriting exercises, or only after you have done them for quite a number of weeks; it may happen frequently or only occasionally; these good bits may be long or short. Everyone's experience is different. But it happens to everyone.

It happens because in those portions of your freewriting that are coherent—in those portions where your mind has somehow gotten into high gear and produced a set of words that grows organically out of a thought or feeling or perception—the integration of meanings is at a finer level than you can achieve by conscious planning or arranging. Sometimes when someone speaks or writes about something that is very important to him, the words he produces have this striking integration or coherence: he isn't having to plan and work them out one by one. They are all permeated by his meaning. The meanings have been blended at a finer level, integrated more thoroughly. Not merely manipulated by his mind, but, rather, sifted through his entire self. In such writing you don't feel mechanical cranking, you don't hear the gears change. When there are transitions they are smooth, natural, organic.

It is as though every word is permeated by the meaning of the whole (like a hologram in which each part contains faintly the whole).

It boils down to something very simple. If you do freewriting regularly, much or most of it will be far inferior to what you can produce through care and rewriting. But the *good* bits will be much better than anything else you can produce by any other method.

KEEP A FREEWRITING DIARY

If you are serious about wanting to improve your writing, the most useful thing you can do is keep a freewriting diary. Just ten minutes a day. Not a complete account of your day; just a brief mind sample for each day. You don't have to think hard or prepare or be in the mood: without stopping, just write whatever words come out—whether or not you are thinking or in the mood.

USING FREEWRITINGS FOR FINDING SUBJECTS TO WRITE ABOUT

Simply do one or two. Afterward, look to see what words or passages seemed important—attracted energy or strength. Here is your cue what to write.

Or think of a person, place, feeling, object, incident, or transaction that is important to you. Do one or two freewriting exercises while trying to hold it in mind. This procedure will suggest a subject and a direction.

PRODUCING A FINISHED PIECE OF WRITING

Keep your topic in mind—or what you think your topic is—and do one or two freewriting exercises. If you are strict with yourself about never stopping for anything, which you must be, then you are likely to wander away from your subject sometimes. This is fine. You will waste energy and weaken your writing if you try to *prevent* digressions before they happen. Let them happen. After they happen, simply find an opportunity to put yourself back on the original subject. But in some cases you will realize that the digression is sufficiently engrossing or important that you should stick with it. Do so.

In either case, after the exercise take a few moments or more to rest and think about what you wrote. Think, too, about the digressions you started and perhaps continued. Notice when they occurred and where they took you. Think about their connections. Consider them as paths you should explore.

Then do another exercise and let these reflections enrich what you are writing. Do this three or more times. Each time you will thus be plowing more and more back into the new exercise. They will become richer. You may well find that your real subject turns out to be something quite different from what you originally thought your subject was. Fine.

After you have done three or four exercises that are more or less "on" what your subject turns out to be, you will have piles of rubble, but you will probably also have a lot of words, phrases, and sentences that seem important. Pick out these good bits. Strip away the rubble. *Now* use as much careful thought and editorial discrimination as possible in order to see what they add up to: decide how much you believe them, how true they are, in what senses they are true; arrange them somehow so they make sense, and write new and connecting parts when necessary.

This may seem a wasteful method. You usually throw away much more than you keep. But for many people, it is really a *quicker, easier* way to produce a *better* short piece of writing.

This method is not foolproof. Sometimes you can only produce rubble—no good bits. This is particularly likely when you first start doing freewriting or during some period of your life in which you are in retreat. Don't be anxious to get something good every time. The main usefulness of the exercises is not in their immediate product but in their gradual effect on future writing.

2

The Process of Writing— Growing

MOST people's relationship to the process of writing is one of helplessness. First, they can't write satisfactorily or even at all. Worse yet, their efforts to improve don't seem to help. It always seems that the amount of effort and energy put into a piece of writing has no relation to the results. People without education say, "If only I had education I could write." People with education say, "If only I had talent I could write." People with education and talent say, "If only I had self-discipline I could write." People with education, talent, and self-discipline—and there are plenty of them who can't write—say, "If only . . ." and don't know what to say next. Yet *some* people who aren't educated, self-disciplined, smart, imaginative, witty (or even verbal, some of them) nevertheless have this peculiar quality most of us lack: when they want to say something or figure something out they can get their thoughts onto paper in a readable form.

My starting point, then, is that the ability to write is unusually mysterious to most people. After all, life is full of difficult tasks: getting up in the morning, playing the piano, learning to play baseball, learning history. But few of them seem so acutely unrelated to effort or talent.

We could solve this mystery like the old "faculty" psychologists and say there is a special "writing faculty" and some people have it and some don't. Or like some linguists, explain what is difficult to explain by saying it's a matter of wiring in the head. Or fall back on the oldest and most popular idea: *inspiration*—some god or muse comes down and breathes into you. Or pretend we don't believe in gods and translate this into some suitably fuzzy equivalent, for example "having something to say": as though certain people at certain times were lucky enough to find "something to say" inside which forced its way out of them onto paper. (And as though people who *can* write are especially distinguished by always having something to say!) In short, we are back to where almost everyone starts: helpless before the process of writing because it obeys inscrutable laws. We are in its power. It is not in ours.

Once there was a land where people felt helpless about trying to touch the floor without bending their knees. Most of them couldn't do it because the accepted doctrine about touching the floor was that you did it by stretching upwards as high as you could. They were confused about the relationship between up and down. The more they tried to touch the floor, reaching up, the more they couldn't do it. But a few people learned accidentally to touch the floor: if they didn't think too much about it they could do it whenever they wanted. But they couldn't explain it to other people because whatever they said didn't make sense. The reaching-up idea of how to touch the floor was so ingrained that even they thought they were reaching up, but in some special way. Also there were a few teachers who got good results: not by telling people how to do it, since that always made things worse, but by getting people to do certain exercises such as tying your shoes without sitting down and shaking your hands around at the same time.

This is the situation with writing. We suffer from such a basic misconception about the process of writing that we are as bad off as the people in the parable.

The commonsense, conventional understanding of writing is as follows. Writing is a two-step process. First you figure out your meaning, then you put it into language. Most advice we get either from others or from ourselves follows this model: first try to figure out what you want to say; don't start writing till you do; make a plan; use an outline; begin writing only afterward. Central to this model is the idea of keeping control, keeping things in hand. Don't let things wander into a mess. The commonest criticism directed at the *process* of writing is that you didn't clarify your thinking ahead of time; you allowed yourself to go ahead with fuzzy thinking; you allowed yourself to wander; you didn't make an outline.

Here is a classic statement of this idea. I copied it from somewhere a long time ago and put it on my wall as something admirable. It was an important day when I finally recognized it as the enemy:

In order to form a good style, the primary rule and condition is, not to attempt to express ourselves in language before we thoroughly know our meaning; when a man perfectly understands himself, appropriate diction will generally be at his command either in writing or speaking.

I contend that virtually all of us carry this model of the writing process around in our heads and that it sabotages our efforts to write. Our knowledge of this model might take the following form if it were put into conscious words: "Of course I can't expect my mess of a mind to follow those two steps perfectly. I'm no writer. But it will help my writing to *try*: by holding off writing and taking time to sit, think, make little jottings, try to figure out what I want to say, and make an outline. In the second step I certainly won't be able to find appropriate diction right at my command but I should try for the best diction I can get: by noticing as often as I can when the diction isn't appropriate, crossing it out, correcting, and trying to write it better."

This idea of writing is backwards. That's why it causes so much trouble. Instead of a two-step transaction of meaning-into-language, think of writing as an organic, developmental process in which you start writing at the very beginning—before you know your meaning at all—and encourage your words gradually to change and evolve. Only at the end will you know what you want to say or the words you want to say it with. You should expect yourself to end up somewhere different from where you started. Meaning is not what you start out with but what you end up with. Control, coherence, and knowing your mind are not what you start out with but what you end up with. Think of writing then not as a way to transmit a message but as a way to grow and cook a message. Writing is a way to end up thinking something you couldn't have started out thinking. Writing is, in fact, a transaction with words whereby you *free* yourself from what you presently think, feel, and perceive. You make available to yourself something better than what you'd be stuck with if you'd actually succeeded in making your meaning clear at the start. What looks inefficient—a rambling process with lots of writing and lots of throwing away—is really efficient since it's the best way you can work up to what you really want to say and how to say it. The real inefficiency is to beat your head against the brick wall of trying to say what you mean or trying to say it well before you are ready.

AUTOBIOGRAPHICAL DIGRESSION

Though much or all of this may be in other books—some of which I have probably read—it seems to me my main source is my own experience. I admit to making universal generalizations upon a sample of one. Consider yourself warned. I am only asking you to *try on* this way of looking at the writing process to see if it helps your writing. That's the only valid way you can judge it. And you will try it on better if you sense how it grows out of my experience.

In high school I wrote relatively easily and—according to those standards—satisfactorily. In college I began to have difficulty writing. Sometimes I wrote badly, sometimes I wrote easily and sometimes with excruciating difficulty. Starting early and planning carefully didn't seem to be the answer: sometimes it seemed to help, sometimes it seemed to make things worse.

Whether or not I succeeded in getting something written seemed related only to whether I screwed myself up into some state of frantic emotional intensity: sometimes about the subject I was writing about; occasionally about some extraneous matter in my life; usually about how overdue the paper was and how frightened I was of turning in nothing at all. There was one term in my junior year when by mistake I signed up for a combination of courses requiring me to write two substantial papers a week. After the first two weeks' crisis, I found I wrote fluently and with relatively little difficulty for the rest of the term. But next term, reality returned. The gods of writing turned their back again.

The saving factor in college was that I wasn't sure whether I cared more about skiing or about studies. But then I went to graduate school and committed myself to studies. This involved deciding to try *very hard* and plan my writing *very carefully*. Writing became more and more impossible. I finally reached the point where I could not write at all. I had to quit graduate school and go into a line of work that didn't require any writing. Teaching English in college wasn't what I had in mind, but it was the only job I could get so it had to do.

After five years I found myself thinking I knew some important things about teaching (not writing!) and wanting badly to get other people to know and believe them. I decided I wanted to write them down and get them published; and also to return to graduate school and get my degree. This time I managed to get myself to write things. I always wondered when the curtain might fall again. I hit on the technique of simply insisting on getting *something* written a week before the real deadline, so I could try to patch it up and make it readable. This worked. But as I watched myself trying to write, it became clear I was going through fantastically inefficient processes. The price I was having to pay for those words was all out of proportion to any real value.

My difficulties in writing, my years as an illiterate English teacher, and a recent habit of trying to keep a stream of consciousness diary whenever life in general got to be too much for me—all combined to make me notice what was happening as I tried to write. I kept a kind of almost-diary. There were two main themes—what I called "stuckpoints" and "breakthroughs." Stuckpoints were when I couldn't get anything written at all no matter how hard I tried: out of pure des-

peration and rage I would finally stop trying to write the
thing and take a fresh sheet of paper and simply try to collect
evidence: babble everything I felt, when it started, and what
kind of writing and mood and weather had been going on.
Breakthroughs were when the log-jam broke and something
good happened: I would often stop and try to say afterwards
what I thought happened. I recommend this practice. If you
keep your own data, you may be able to build your own
theory of how *you* can succeed in writing since my theory of
how I can succeed may not work for you. This chapter and
the next one grow to some extent out of these jottings. Occasionally I will quote from them.

IT MAKES A DIFFERENCE IN PRACTICE

In a sense I have nothing to offer but two metaphors: *growing*
and *cooking*. They are my model for the writing process. But
models and metaphors make a big difference—most of all,
those models and metaphors we take for granted.

Before going on to describe the model in detail, therefore,
I would like to give a concrete example, and contrast the way
you might normally go about a typical writing task and how
you might go about doing it if you adopted the developmental
model.

Imagine writing something three to five pages long and
fairly difficult. It's not something you have to research (or
else you've already done the research), but you haven't really
worked out what you want to say. Perhaps it is a school essay.
Or perhaps it is a short story for which you have an idea but
no sense yet of how to work it out. To make the clearest contrast between the two ways of writing, let's say that you can
only give one evening to the job.

If you wrote this normally, you would probably write it more or less once, but as carefully as possible. That is, you would probably spend anywhere from 15 minutes to an hour on planning: thinking, jotting, making an outline, or all three. And you would try hard to leave yourself at least half an hour at the end to go back over it and make clarifications and changes: usually while copying it over. Thus, though there may be a lot of "getting ready" beforehand, and "fixing" afterwards, you are essentially writing it *once*. And while you are doing the writing itself you probably do a lot of stopping, thinking, crossing out, going back, rewriting: everything that's involved in trying to write it as well as you can.

If on the other hand you adopt the developmental model of the writing process, you might well try to write it four times, not once, and try to help the piece evolve through these four versions. This sounds crazy and impossible because the writing process is usually so slow and tortured, but it needn't be. You simply have to force yourself to write. Of course the first "version" won't really be a version. It will simply be a writing down in the allotted time of everything on your mind concerning the subject.

Suppose you have four hours. Divide it into four units of *e. g.* an hour. For the first 45 minutes, simply write as quickly as you can, as though you were talking to someone. All the things that come to mind about the matter. You may not be able to write everything you know in that time, or you may have written everything you know in the first 10 minutes. Simply keep writing in either case—thinking things out as the words go down onto paper, following your train of thought where it leads, following the words where they lead. But stop at the end of 45 minutes.

Take the last 15 minutes for the opposite process. Think

back or read over what you have written and try to see what important things emerged. What does it add up to? What was the most important or central thing in it? *Make* it add up to something, try to guess what it's *trying* to add up to; try to figure out what it *would* add up to if the missing parts were there. Sum up this main point, this incipient center of gravity, in a sentence. Write it down. It's got to stick its neck out, not just hedge or wonder. Something that can be quarreled with. (If you are writing a story or poem stress the term "center of gravity": it may be an assertion, but it could also be a mood, an image, a central detail or event or object—as long as it somehow sums up everything.) This summing-up process should be difficult: it should tell you more than you already know.

Of course you probably can't come up at this point with an assertion that is true or pleasing. You probably can't even make an assertion that really fits everything you wrote for 45 minutes. Don't worry. Your job, as with the writing, is not to do the task well, it is to do the task. The essence of this approach is to change your notion of what it means to *try* or *attempt* or *work on* a piece of writing. To most people it means pushing as hard as they can against a weight that is heavier than they can budge—hoping eventually to move it. Whereas of course you merely get tireder. You must create mechanical advantage so that "trying" means pushing against a weight that you *can* move even if that only moves the main weight a small distance.

So now you have used up the first of your four units of time. You have written your first "version." In the next hour, simply do the same thing. Start writing again. *Start from* your previous summing up assertion. That doesn't mean you must stick to it—you probably consider it false. Merely write your next version "in the light of" or "from the perspective of" your fifteen-minute standing back and surveying of the terrain.

Write quickly without much stopping and correcting for 45 minutes again. And again use the final 15 minutes to stand back and try to see what emerged, what one thing is now uppermost or is trying to be uppermost. Sum it up again. Perhaps this assertion will seem solider and more useful, but perhaps not. In any event, you must come up with a single, sticking-its-neck-out assertion by the end of 15 minutes.

Now in your third hour do the same thing a third time. By now you may have a sense of which direction your final version will go—a sense of an emerging center of gravity that you trust. Try to develop and exploit it. If not, try to find it during this third version. Try to coax some coherence, yet still allow things to bubble. You are not editing yet.

The job of editing and turning out a final copy is next. It occupies the last 15 minutes of your third period, and the whole of the fourth period. It turns out to be exactly what the conventional idea of writing is: start with 15 minutes to make your meaning clear to yourself. Now at last you should be in a position to do this. You might want to make an outline or plan. But one thing is essential: you must really force yourself to sum up into a genuine *single* assertion what your meaning is. Remember the crucial thing about this task: it must be an assertion that actually asserts something, that could be quarrelled with; not "here are some things I think" or "here are some things that relate to X."

Once you have gradually grown your meaning and specified it to yourself clearly, you *will* have an easier time finding the best language for it. But even in this final writing, don't go too slowly and carefully. For you should use the final 15 minutes for going over it: cleaning and strengthening the wording; throwing away as many words, phrases, and even sections as can be dispensed with; and perhaps rearranging some parts.

This method of writing means more words written and thrown away. Perhaps even more work. But less banging your head against a stone wall—pushing with all your might against something that won't budge. So though you are tired, you are less frustrated. The process tends to create a transaction that helps you expend more of your energy more productively.

The time-lengths can be stretched or squeezed or ignored. I am merely trying to insist that you can write much more and not take longer. But most of us must resort to a clock to *make* ourselves write more and not waste time.

GROWING

Growing is certainly a proper word for what people and other living organisms do to arrive at a "grown" or "mature" state. They go through a series of changes and end up more complex and organized than when they started. It is no metaphor to speak of a person in the following way: "He really grew. Of course he's the same person he was, but he's also very different. Now he thinks, behaves, and sees things differently from the way he used to. I never would have expected him to end up this way."

I wish to speak of groups of *words* growing in the same way. Consider this example. You believe X. You write out your belief or perception or argument that X is the case. By the time you have finished you see something you didn't see before: X is incorrect or you see you no longer believe X. Now you keep writing about your perplexity and uncertainty.

Then you begin to see Y. You start to write about Y. You finally see that Y is correct or you believe Y. And then finally you write out Y as fully as you can and you are satisfied with it.

What has happened here? Strictly speaking, only *you* have grown, your words have not. You are a living organism. Your words are just dead marks on a piece of paper. No word has *moved* or *changed,* they all just lie there where you set them. But there's a sense in which they have changed. A sense in which they are not one long string of words but rather three shorter strings of words which are three "versions" of something: versions of an organism-like thing—something that has gone through three stages and ended up in a way that seems completed. "It no longer believes X, it believes Y; it's very different, yet it's still the same piece of writing. I never would have expected it to end up this way."

It is my experience that when I write something that is good or which satisfies me, almost invariably it is a product of just such a process. And when I struggle hard and fail to produce something good or pleasing, it seems almost invariably because I couldn't get this kind of process to occur. (There are exceptions which I will deal with towards the end of the chapter on cooking.)

It is also my experience that I can best help this process occur when I think of it as trying to "help words grow." It is true, of course, that an initial set of words does not, like a young live organism, contain within each cell a *plan* for the final mature stage and all the intervening stages that must be gone through. Perhaps, therefore, the final higher organization in the words should only be called a borrowed reflection of a higher organization that is really in me or my mind. I am only projecting. Yet nevertheless, when I can write down a

set of words and then write down some more and then go
back and write down some more thoughts or perceptions on
the topic, two odd things seem to be the case: 1. Often by
looking back over them, I can find relationships and conclusions in the words that are far richer and more interesting
than I could have "thought of by myself." 2. And sometimes
it often feels as though these words were "going somewhere"
such that when they "got there" best, it was because I succeeded in getting out of their way. It seems not entirely metaphorical, then, to say that at the end it is I who have borrowed
some higher organization from the words.

In any event, I advise you to treat words as though they are
potentially able to grow. Learn to stand out of the way and
provide the energy or force the words need to find their growth
process. The words cannot go against entropy and end up
more highly organized than when they started unless fueled by
energy you provide. You must send that energy or electricity
through the words in order, as it were, to charge them or ionize
them or give them juice or whatever so that they have the life
to go through the growing process. I think of this growing
process schematically, as follows. The words come together
into one pile and interact with each other in that mess; then
they come apart into small piles according to some emerging
pattern. Then the small piles consolidate and shake down into
their own best organization. Then together again into a big
pile where everything interacts and bounces off everything else
till a different pattern emerges. The big pile breaks up again
into different parts according to this new pattern. Then the
parts each consolidate themselves again. Then back into the
big pile again for more interaction. And so forth and so on till
it's "over"—till a pattern or configuration is attained that
pleases you or that "it was trying to get to."

It takes a lot of energy for this process to go on. But you save the energy you normally waste trying to polish something that is essentially lousy and undeveloped.

Make the process of writing into atomic fission, setting off a chain reaction, putting things into a pot to percolate, getting words to take on a life of their own. Writing is like trying to ride a horse which is constantly changing beneath you, Proteus changing while you hang on to him. You have to hang on for dear life, but not hang on so hard that he can't change and finally tell you the truth.

In the following sections I try to describe the growing process more concretely in four stages: start writing and keep writing; disorientation and chaos; emerging center of gravity; mopping up or editing.

START WRITING AND KEEP WRITING

It is one of the main functions of the ten-minute writing exercises to give you practice in writing quickly without editing, for if you are not used to it you will find it difficult. Your editorial instinct is often much better developed than your producing instinct, so that as each phrase starts to roll off your pencil, you hear seventeen reasons why it is unsatisfactory. The paper remains blank. Or else there are a series of crossed out half-sentences and half-paragraphs.

When you realize you have to write a lot, you stop worrying because you write badly much of the time—at first, perhaps all the time. Don't worry. "Trying to write well" for most people means constantly stopping, pondering, and searching for better words. If this is true of you, then stop "trying to write well." Otherwise you will never write well.

It's at the beginnings of things that you most need to get yourself to write a lot and fast. Beginnings are hardest: the beginning of a sentence, of a paragraph, of a section, of a stanza, of a whole piece. This is when you spend the most time not-writing: sitting, staring off into space, chewing the pencil, furrowing your brow, feeling stuck. How can you write the beginning of something till you know what it's the beginning of? Till you know what it's leading up to? But how can you know that till you get your beginnings?

Writing is founded on these impossible double-binds. It is simply a fact that most of the time you can't find the right words till you know exactly what you are saying, but that you can't know exactly what you are saying till you find just the right words. The consequence is that you must *start by writing the wrong meanings in the wrong words;* but keep writing till you get to the right meanings in the right words. Only at the end will you know what you are saying. Here is a diary entry:

Noticing it again: in the middle of writing a memo to X about the course: that the good ideas and good phrases—especially the good ideas—come only while in the process of writing—after the juices have started to flow. It's what Macrorie[1] is talking about when he says you have to let words talk to words—let words—as they come out—call up and suggest other words and concepts and analogies. There's a very practical moral for me. I've got to *not* expect my best or even structurally important ideas to come before I start writing. Got to stop worrying that I have nothing to write about before I start writing. Start to write and let things happen. A model: pretend I am a famous writer—an acknowledged genius who has already produced a brilliant book a year and an article a month for the last 20 years. Someone who simply knows that when he sits down to write, good stuff will be the final

1. Ken Macrorie, *Telling Writing*, Hayden Press, 1970.

product even though at any given moment he is liable to be writing absolute crap. Good writers and good athletes don't get really good till they stop worrying and hang loose and trust that good stuff will come. Good musicians.

Writing a lot at the beginning is also important because that's when you are least warmed up and most anxious. Anxiety keeps you from writing. You don't know what you will end up writing. Will it be enough? Will it be any good? You begin to think of critical readers and how they will react. You get worried and your mind begins to cloud. You start trying to clench your mind around what pitiful little lumps of material you have in your head so as not to lose them. But as you try to clarify one thought, all the rest seem to fall apart. It's like trying to play monopoly on a hillside in a fresh breeze and trying to keep a hand on all your piles of money. You begin to wonder whether you are coming down with a brain tumor. Anxiety is trying to get you so stuck and disgusted that you stop writing altogether. It is writing that causes all the anxiety. (When you have dreams of glory and imagine how famous your writing will make you, it is just a sneakier trick to keep you from writing: anything you actually write will seem disappointing to you.)

Again, the only cure is to damn the torpedoes and write:

Getting into the teacher business in my "Model for Higher Education" essay. Beginning to turn on. Lesson: two conditions seem to have led to this more gutsy writing. 1. Write a lot for enough time just to get tired and get into it—get past stiffness and awkwardness—like in a cross-country race where your technique doesn't get good till you're genuinely tired. The mechanism there is clear: you've got to be tired enough so that unnecessary (and inhibitory) muscles let go and stop clenching. Relax. Use only necessary muscles. Reach 100% efficiency of body. Equals grace. I think you can translate this directly into writing: get extra and inhibitory muscles to let go by writing a lot. Thus the success of some late-night writing. 2. I've found or fallen into a topic that I have a strong emotional relation to. It's got my dander up. I can feel it in my stomach and arms and jaw—which in this case doesn't feel like unnecessary and inhibitory muscle tension. You have to write long enough, get tired enough, and drift and wander and *digress* enough simply to fall into an area of high concern. *The whole thing started out as a digression: one parenthesis for one sentence in a section talking about something entirely different.* Give your feelings and instincts their head.

Trying to begin is like being a little child who cannot write on unlined paper. I cannot write anything decent or interesting until after I have written something at least as long as the thing I want to end up with. I go back over it and cross it all out or throw it all away, but it operates as a set of lines that hold me up when I write, something to warm up the paper so my ink will "take," a security blanket. Producing writing, then, is not so much like filling a basin or pool once, but rather getting water to keep flowing *through* till finally it runs clear. What follows is a diary entry that starts out illustrating the need to write beginnings and get on with it, but ends up showing that the problem of anxiety tends to lurk underneath everything else:

I've stopped in mid sentence. I'm starting off this long section; and I realize that exactly what I need at this point is a clear and concise summary statement of precisely what it is I'm going to say. And with that realization comes a trickier one: I cannot say clearly and concisely what it all amounts to.
The best I can do is write in something vague or fuzzy or unsatisfactory—to fake it like a musician who comes to a passage that is too hard but wants to keep time with the other players and not lose his place in the music—and go on to the substance of the sec-

tion to work out exactly what it is I *am* saying. I cannot write the sentence I need at the beginning till after I get to the end.

The lesson, then, is to try to treat writing not exclusively as linear but as wholistic: not starting in at one end and writing till you get to the other; but rather as successive sketches of the same picture—the first sketches very rough and vague—each one getting clearer, more detailed, more accurate, and better organized as well.

And different parts of the writing must have a mutually interactive effect on each other. I can't write a good first sentence till I work through the body of the piece; yet once I work through the body and get myself in a position of elevation so I can write a good first sentence summarizing things, that very sentence will permit me to go back to the body of the piece and see that some bits are not really central and can be cut out or shortened or stuck into a quick aside; and bring the main outlines into better focus.

But. Now after writing the above, I went back to my piece of writing, and succeeded pretty well in putting my finger on what it was I was wanting to say. Somehow the stopping and making self-conscious the process outlined above, served to free me from the hangup of it. I don't know how to translate that into advice or a general principle. Wait a minute, maybe I do. I think it means this: *I was stuck and frustrated,* couldn't go on. Became conscious of it and what the problem was. Stopped to make a note analyzing the problem and the solution. And that produced confidence that the problem did indeed have a solution—reduced the frustration—know that if I just forged on bravely, it would eventually come to me. That reduction of frustration and incipient hopelessness reduced the static in my mind that was preventing me from getting my hands on words and thoughts that were potentially there.

Another reason for starting writing and keeping writing: If you stop too much and worry and correct and edit, you'll invest yourself too much in these words on the page. You'll care too much about them; you'll make some phrases you really love; you won't be able to throw them away. But you *should* throw lots away because by the end you'll have a different focus or angle on what you are writing, if not a whole new subject. To keep these earlier words would ruin your final product. It's like scaffolding. There is no shortcut by which you can avoid building it, even though it can't be part of your final building. It's like the famous recipe for sturgeon: soak it in vinegar, nail it to a two-inch plank, put it in a slow oven for three days, take it out, throw away the fish, and eat the plank.

It's just happened again. For the umteenth time. I struggled at huge and agonizing length to try to get rid of an unwieldy, ugly, and awkward phrasing. No matter how much I struggled, I couldn't get anything either clear, concise, or even exactly what I meant. But still to no avail. The hell with it. I took the best alternative—a lousy one—and went on. Only the *next day—after typing the final draft—while proofreading it—*I finally got the perfect phrasing: just what I want; elegant, concise, direct. Cognitively, I couldn't work it out till I had the whole thing clear enough so that I could then see this tiny part clearly. Affectively, I couldn't get the cobwebs out of my head till I actually had confidence that I had something actually completed and that I could turn in. Moral: it was a waste of time to try for the exact phrase back then; wait till later—last stage.

CHAOS AND DISORIENTATION

If the main advice people need to help make their writing grow is to start writing and keep writing, their main experience in trying to follow this advice is the feeling of chaos and disorientation. Here is a diary entry from an early stage of working on this book:

I just realized why I'm going crazy. Why I'm starting and stopping in despair. Over and over again. It's so terrible. Finally realize what I'm feeling. *I can't stand writing when I don't know what I'm writing about!* It feels so insecure. Such a mess. Don't know where it's going or coming from. Just writing off into the blue. I'm wanting a center of gravity. But I'm just starting. Can't know what the center of gravity is yet. Got to put up with it. It won't come till the end.

Or here's another one where, like the last one, I know perfectly well the *theory* that I should write a lot and I'm trying to follow it, but I'm discovering how threatening it is in practice. Here I start out, as it were, whistling in the dark by telling myself the theory very confidently; finally I build up the courage to speak to myself of my insecurity:

My main wholistic advice. Process. Write a lot and throw a lot away. Start writing early so you can have time to discard a lot and have it metamorphose a lot and bubble and percolate. If you have 3 hours for a 3-page thing, write it three times instead of one page an hour.
Yet. Yet. I find this hard. I keep trying to hold off actual writing till everything is *perfectly* prepared and totally under control so that I know what I'm going to write. It makes me so nervous to start in writing. I keep putting it off, more and more preparation. It feels like having to jump into cold water.
Whereas when I *do* get writing, I discover that much of the preparation time was a *waste of time.* The important things happen *during* writing; after a first draft; trying to clean it up or reconcile contradictions; or on the way from the third to the fourth draft. I know this from my past experience and from my theory of the writing process. But still I stand here on the edge and don't want to start writing; I prefer to sit here and ponder and think and look through jottings I've made—even write out a diary entry.

The reason it feels like chaos and disorientation to write freely is because you are giving up a good deal of control. You

are allowing yourself to proceed without a full plan—or allowing yourself to depart from whatever plan you have. You are
trying to let the words, thoughts, feelings, and perceptions try
to find some of their own order, logic, coherence. You're trying to get your material to do some of the steering instead of
doing it all yourself.

Growth in writing is not just producing masses of words
and then throwing the rejects away. That could be a simpli-
fied two-step version for getting your feet wet, perhaps, but it
misses out on the essential process. If all you have at the end is
a subset of the words you started with, you have missed real
growth. Things have actually got to *change,* and you will experience this as chaos even if your material, while going
through changes, happens at every moment to be completely
coherent—like a fetus in a mother's belly. The words are not
going through stages *you* planned or that *you* control.

There is a paradox about control which this kind of writing
brings into the open. The common model of writing I grew
up with preaches control. It tells me to think first, make up
my mind what I really mean, figure out ahead of time where
I am going, have a plan, an outline, don't dither, don't be
ambiguous, be stern with myself, don't let things get out of
hand. As I begin to try to follow this advice, I experience a
sense of satisfaction and control: "I'm going to be in charge of
this thing and keep out of any swamps!" Yet almost always
my main experience ends up one of *not* being in control, feeling stuck, feeling lost, trying to write something and never
succeeding. Helplessness and passivity.

The developmental model, on the other hand, preaches, in
a sense, *lack* of control: don't worry about knowing what you
mean or what you intend ahead of time; you don't need a
plan or an outline, let things get out of hand, let things wan-

der and digress. Though this approach makes for initial panic, my overall experience with it is increased control. Not that I always know what I am doing, not that I don't feel lost, baffled, and frustrated. But the overall process is one that doesn't leave me so helpless. I can get something written when I want to. There isn't such a sense of mystery, of randomness.

This paradox of increased overall control through letting go a bit seems paradoxical only because our normal way of thinking about control is mistakenly static: it is not developmental or process-oriented because it leaves out the dimension of time. Our static way of thinking makes us feel we must make a *single* choice as to whether to be a controlled person or an out-of-control person. The feeling goes like this: "Ugh. If I just write words as they come, allow myself to write without a plan or an outline, allow myself to digress or wander, I'll turn into a blithering idiot. I'll degenerate. I'll lose the control I've struggled so hard to get. First I'll dangle participles, then I'll split infinitives, then I'll misspell words, then I'll slide into disagreement of subject and verb. Soon I'll be unable to think straight. Unable to find flaws in an argument. Unable to tell a good argument from a bad one. Unable to tell sound evidence from phony evidence. My mind will grow soft and limp, it will atrophy; it will finally fall off. No! I'll be tough. I won't be wishy-washy. I'll have high standards. I'll be rigorous. I'll make every argument really stand up. I won't be a second-rate mind. I'm going to be a *discriminating* person. I'm going to keep my mind *sharp* at all times."

But this static model isn't accurate. Most processes engaged in by live organisms are cyclic, developmental processes that run through time and end up different from how they began. The fact is that most people find they *improve* their ability to think carefully and discriminatingly if they allow themselves to be sloppy and relinquish control at other times. You usually cannot excel at being toughminded and discriminating unless it is the final stage in an organic process that allowed you to be truly open, accepting—even at times blithering.

You can encourage richness and chaos by encouraging digressions. We often see digressions as a waste of time and break them off when we catch ourselves starting one. But do the opposite. Give it its head. It may turn out to be an integral part of what you are trying to write. Even if it turns out to be an excrescence to be gotten rid of, if it came to you while you were thinking about X it must be related and a source of leverage. And you may not be able to *get rid of it* completely unless you see more of it. Almost always you cannot disentangle the good insight from the excrescence until *after* you have allowed the digression to develop. At the early stage the two are so intertwined that you can't tell one from the other. That's why it feels both interesting and wrong. There are concepts in there that you haven't yet learned to discriminate.

If you allow yourself to get genuinely off the subject you can see it differently when you come back. Even if the digression doesn't turn out to be valuable to what you are writing, it may be valuable in itself. You often have your best ideas about Y when you are thinking about X. If you have to write two things, don't finish one and then start the other: get them both started and work on one for a while and then work on the other. Let them reflect heat on each other like logs in a fireplace.

Using diary entries for this book showed me how chaos can be less chaotic than it seems. I was struck by how much easier it was to fix these carelessly written diary entries than to fix

many troublesome passages that I'd written with more effort
and care. At first glance the diary entries seemed much more
chaotic: often hard to decipher, full of mistakes and changes
of gear in mid-sentence. But a few slight changes—usually a
matter of breaking each longer structure up into two or three
sentences—and they came out simple and clear if not elegant.
In contrast, the more careful passages seemed more coherent:
though too muddy, heavy, or wordy, they were correct and
decipherable. But when I try to make them simple and clear
it is much much harder. In short the stream-of-consciousness
diary entries, though they look on the surface like more of a
mess, are really closer to strong coherence than the more carefully written sentences.

Insisting on control, having a plan or outline, and always
sticking to it is a prophylactic against organic growth, development, change. But it is also a prophylactic against the experience of chaos and disorientation which are very frightening.

EMERGING CENTER OF GRAVITY

The turning point in the whole cycle of growing is the emer-
gence of a focus or a theme. It is also the most mysterious and
difficult kind of cognitive event to analyze. It is the moment
when what was chaos is now seen as having a center of gravity.
There is a shape where a moment ago there was none.

If you are having difficulty getting a center of gravity to
emerge, the cure is to force yourself to make lots of summings-
up even if they don't fit your material or seem to be right. In
effect these early summings-up *are* centers of gravity but because they are so bad they don't feel like centers of gravity.

Getting order to appear in chaos takes practice. First you do it badly, gradually you do it better. If you refrain from doing it badly, you will never learn to do it at all.

What this means in practice is that in a piece of writing you must force yourself to keep getting *some* center of gravity or summing-up to occur. Let the early ones be terrible. They will distort your material by exaggerating some aspects and ignoring others. Fine. If possible, try for contrasting exaggerations. Exaggerating helps you think of things you wouldn't think of if you tried to be judicious. If you keep doing this you will finally evolve toward the more satisfactory position which earlier you couldn't get hold of. Finally you will have a center of gravity that satisfies you. Moderate views limit your horizons; trying to compromise muddles your head. Work gradually toward moderation from extreme positions. If a poem or story has no focus, try giving it exaggerated ones.

It may help if I list some ways in which a center of gravity emerged for me:

1. Simple reversal: starting to write X and seeing, through development of X, that Y is right. I couldn't get there directly. I remember I had even considered Y first, but I hadn't believed it. I had to go through X first before I could really understand Y.

2. Struggling back and forth between X and Y and coming up with Z. Not possible by a shorter cut.

3. Writing along and suddenly saying, "Ah! *Now* I see what I've been getting at."

4. Not seeing the point of what I had written till much later. Wrote the whole thing. Only after it was completely finished—or at least I thought it was all finished—and after putting it aside for some time, could I finally see that it

implied something I hadn't yet understood. It was so obvious then, but I couldn't see it earlier.

5. Having what seems like a good idea. Being very fond of it. But then seeing it as crap. Having nothing left, it seemed. Then finally seeing that there are some *parts* of the "good idea" that are good (or some senses in which it is true) and some parts bad. But I couldn't sort it out earlier. It had looked like only one idea. I didn't see it had parts. I felt I had either to throw it all away or endorse it completely. But by interaction with other, conflicting ideas, I was finally able to discriminate parts of the original idea and salvage the good parts and discard the others. Once I could make this discrimination, it seemed so natural: those good parts were so much better than that original "favorite idea."

6. Scaffolding. Writing X. It seems great. But then I find next day that it seems mediocre. But further writing produces an extension of it. That's better. The original was scaffolding that I had to use to get to the second one. Then throw it away.

7. Parentheses, digression, subset. Some little detail in what I was writing, perhaps just an image or phrase or parenthesis, seems to have a spark to it. I let it go and it ends up being the main point, the center of gravity. And what I had thought was the center of gravity turns out to be only a subsidiary part. The whole thing drastically changes its orientation. Even though most of the same elements are still there, it feels very different.

this is it same discussion today w/ Dr Kriss

June 96

EDITING

You can't edit till you have something to edit. If you have written a lot, if you have digressed and wandered into some interesting areas and accumulated some interesting material (more than you can see any unity in), and if, at last, a center of gravity has emerged and you find yourself finally saying to yourself, "Yes, now I see what I'm driving at, now I see what I've been stumbling around trying to say," you are finally in a position to start mopping up—to start editing.

Editing means figuring out what you really mean to say, getting it clear in your head, getting it unified, getting it into an organized structure, and then getting it into the best words and throwing away the rest. It is crucial, but it is only the last step in the complete growth cycle.

Sometimes you can get a piece of writing to go through the whole cycle so naturally that even this last stage performs itself: you have written it, written it, and written it some more, and finally you find yourself writing it right. You simply throw away the first fifteen pages and keep the last three because they are just what you want.

This rarely happens with a whole piece of writing, but it often happens with sections: paragraphs or stanzas can come right off the end of your pencil just the way you want them. Look for it and want it. But usually you are writing something for tomorrow or next week and a completely natural growth cycle often takes longer.

Editing is almost invariably manipulative, intrusive, artificial, and compromising: red-penciling, cutting up, throwing away, rewriting. And mostly throwing away. For this process, follow all the standard advice about writing: be vigilant, ruthless; be orderly, planned; keep control, don't lose your head. At last it is appropriate to sit, ponder, furrow your brow, not write, try to think of a better word, struggle for the exact phrase, try to cut out "dead wood," make up your mind what you really mean: all the activities which ruin your writing if engaged in too soon.

Sometimes I don't need to use an outline to do a good job of editing. But if I get the least bit stuck—knowing that it's not right but not sure what's wrong—then I find an outline indispensable: but only at this last stage of writing, not at early stages.

I used to think outlines were made of single words and phrases. But I found that's not good enough. I found the only effective outline to be a list of full assertions—one for each paragraph. Each must assert something definite, not just point in a general direction. Then the *progression* of assertions must make sense and say something so you can finally force that list of assertions into a *single* assertion that really says something. And now, having worked your way up, you can work your way down again to clean and tighten things up: with this single assertion, you can now reorder your list of paragraph assertions into a tighter order (probably leaving some out); and only now can you finally rewrite your actual paragraphs so they all reflect in their texture—at the cellular level —the single coherence of the whole piece.

The essence of editing is *easy come easy go*. Unless you can really say to yourself, "What the hell. There's plenty more where that came from, let's throw it away," you can't really edit. You have to be a big spender. Not tightass.

I am the first to admit how hard it is to practice this preaching. I *know* perfectly well I can write an infinite number of meaningful utterances in my native tongue in spite of my

finite knowledge of that language. I *know* perfectly well that
the more I utter, the more I'll be able to utter and—other
things being equal—the *better* I'll be able to utter. I know I
can. Noam Chomsky knows I can. But it doesn't *feel* that way.
It feels like the more I utter, especially the more I write, the
more I'll use up my supply of meaningful utterances, and as
the source dries up, they will get worse.

What is illustrated here is the essence of the developmental
growth cycle for living cells. A difficulty in a later stage (editing) reveals a hitherto unnoticed difficulty at an earlier stage
(producing). Progress is liable to require regression: experiencing the earlier stage difficulty more fully so it can be
worked on. Or at least this is how it worked for me. I had
figured out perfectly well the importance of writing a lot and
producing a lot, but not until I began to see more clearly my
difficulties with editing did I realize that I was being held up
because I hadn't *really* inhabited fully my difficulties with
producing. A relatively recent diary entry:

I'm reading over something I wrote a couple of days ago. Trying
to turn it into a final draft. I was working on the phrase, "There
is no principle of right or wrong, and no guidelines for trying to
sort it out or bring consistency to it." I could feel immediately
that it was wordy and mushy; fog for the reader. Next I find myself rewriting it as follows: "There's no right or wrong for sorting
it out; no guidelines for bringing consistency." Yes, that's better,
I start to say to myself, when I suddenly realize what I'm really
doing. I'm working out a recombination of the words *in order
not to have to throw any of them away.* I've done it a million
times, but this is the first time I can feel the psychic principle in
it: "How can I rearrange those words in order not to throw any
of them away? I made those words. All by myself. They came out
of me. And it was hell. I really suffered. I gave them my everything. For each word there were 17 traps and pitfalls that I just

barely avoided by my sharp-eyed vigilance, 17 agonizing choices, 17 near-misses. I struggled. I ain't getting rid of any of them. Get out of here with that knife."

Now that I have stressed the developmental fact that learning to throw away more ruthlessly comes from learning to generate more prolificly—that learning how to impose higher degrees of organization comes from allowing more disorder— I can go on to stress the fierceness of editing. For that's the difficulty of most advice about writing: because it doesn't do justice to the earlier, nonediting stages in the writing process, it doesn't *really* do justice to editing.

Editing must be cut-throat. You must wade in with teeth gritted. Cut away flesh and leave only bone. Learn to say things with a relationship instead of words. If you have to make introductions or transitions, you have things in the wrong order. If they were in the right order they wouldn't need introductions or transitions. Force yourself to leave out all subsidiaries and then, by brute force, you will have to re-arrange the essentials into their proper order.

Every word omitted keeps another reader with you. Every word retained saps strength from the others. Think of throwing away not as negative—not as crumpling up sheets of paper in helplessness and rage—but as a positive, creative, generative act. Learn to play the role of the sculptor pulling off layers of stone with his chisel to reveal a figure beneath. Leaving things out makes the backbone or structure show better.

Try to *feel* the act of strength in the act of cutting: as you draw the pencil through the line or paragraph or whole page, it is a clenching of teeth to make a point stick out more, hit home harder. Conversely, try to feel that when you write in a mushy, foggy, wordy way, you must be trying to cover something up: message-emasculation or self-emasculation. You

must be afraid of your strength. Taking away words lets a
loud voice stick out. Does it scare you? More words will cover
it up with static. It is no accident that timid people are often
wordy. Saying nothing takes guts. If you want to say nothing
and not be noticed, you have to be wordy.

Editing means being tough enough to make sure someone
will actually read it:

Don't look on throwing words away as something having gone
wrong. To write ten pages and throw them away but end up
with *one paragraph* that someone actually reads—*one paragraph
that is actually worth sixty seconds of someone's time*—is a huge
and magical and efficient process. The alternative which is much
more common is to write (more carefully) five pages that *avoid the
errors or egregious shit* of the above ten pages—*but not one single
paragraph worth reading!* So though it seems that one has done
better when one has five whole pages of non-shit, really it is
utterly worthless since it's not worth reading.

In all three previous stages of growth, the emphasis is upon
a transaction with yourself and with your words. In editing,
you must finally deal with the hard reality of readers.

GROWING AS A DEVELOPMENTAL PROCESS

If you want to adopt this approach to writing, there is no easy
set of rules to follow. At different stages in the writing process
you should be doing opposite things. And it is not always easy
to know what stage you are at. No two pieces of writing, no
two pieces of organic growth, will be exactly alike. And of
course I may have some of it wrong here—or my growth cycle
may be somewhat different from yours. Thus the main thing
you must do if you want to help growing happen in your writ-

ing is to try to get a feel for the organic, developmental process. This means trying to get the feeling of a shape in the dimension of time—the shape of a set of changes occurring in a structure.

I first got the feeling for this model a few years ago when I was writing something that was very important to me. I had a lot of notes for it that contained everything I wanted to say. But these notes were jotted down over a period of weeks and were a random mess. I had to work hard for a full week or so trying to write these ideas up into something coherent. At the end I looked back at my original notes to see if I'd forgotten anything important. What struck me was how different and inferior they were. I had thought that everything in the paper was in the notes. But now as I looked back at the notes I saw they had a limited, different, and amazingly unuseful point of view. I suddenly realized that it was like looking back on something I'd written a couple of years ago: yes those were my ideas and my present ideas are related, but they've grown. In short I realized that in this intensive period of writing and throwing away and writing, it was as though I had succeeded in accelerating the passage of time and hastening the growth process.

It is the characteristic of living organisms, cell creatures, to unfold according to a set of stages that must come in order. The paradigm is the fetus going through all its stages. Freud's contribution is a developmental model for psychic unfolding: the organism must go through oral, anal, and genital stages of development. Erik Erikson makes a seven-stage model. Piaget makes a developmental model for cognitive growth.[2]

2. William Perry and his associates have a good book on the developmental process in college students: *Intellectual and Emotional Development in the College Years*, 1970.

The developmental model explains a lot about human affairs and makes many paradoxes come clear. The main thing is that these stages must all be gone through in order. None may be skipped. A person is held back from attaining a certain stage if he hasn't completed or done justice to some previous stage (even though it may not show on the surface). This means that if you are having difficulty becoming something, you ought to look to see if there isn't something you used to be that you haven't really finished being; or something you tried to skip. Have you been pretending or trying from the neck up to live at a later stage than you are really at? You probably have to allow yourself to *be* or *inhabit* this earlier stage more genuinely—without hedging or crossing your fingers behind your back. I think of the advice of Krishnamurti to a school child troubled by laziness: he says maybe the child isn't lazy *enough*.

Thus in writing, your words must go through stages. There are no shortcuts. (Though not every stage is necessarily overt: more about this under *Cooking*.) The stages may be gone through more quickly if you can muster the energy to have more experience per hour.

You will be tired, of course. But you will save some of the other kinds of energy that are so often wasted in writing. For from here we can see one of the main sources of frustration and despair in writing: trying to make the first version any good. One struggles to improve it and fix it. But really it can't be any good. It's got to be abandoned and moved past. Probably the second one too. And so the point is not to waste more time on it than is needed. Sketch it in roughly; move fast; not too much investment or commitment.

But there is a tricky line here. For you must spend *enough* time and effort to actually have it be a kind of version. You can't actually *skip* it. Otherwise you are back in the original dead end: fooling around a little at the start but essentially trying to beat the development process and make your first version your last one—trying to skip adolescence again.

The developmental model gives an understanding of my main stuckpoint: again and again I start to move toward X; but then I feel it is no good; stop; try to see what a new idea or center of gravity is; I see Y; try that for a while, but then feel that there's something really bad about it; then the same for Z. And then here I am at my main stuckpoint. I feel caught in a great swamp. The moment I try to move toward X, Y, or Z, I see that each is no good. But I can't think of any more. I keep trying them and abandoning them over and over again. Get more and more tired, discouraged, head-swimming.

The problem is that I'm not taking any of them far enough. I let myself get stopped by feelings of wrongness. My critical and editorial instinct has rumbled into action too soon. For I've discovered that when I force myself to take one of those paths—it doesn't much matter whether I choose X, Y, or Z— and really develop that train of thought fully towards its end, it gets me out of the swamp. I have to *force* myself to do it against the horrible feeling that it is a waste of time. And usually it is indeed wrong. But I was caught in the swamp because I didn't allow it to *be* fully X, Y, or Z. And once I do— not of course writing out a fully polished draft—perhaps following it in a very sketchy way, roughly, hurriedly, *but to its end*—then I see a whole new direction to go in that I couldn't see before. (Or see how X, Y, or Z is indeed right.) I couldn't see it till I'd let the writing *be* one of its earlier stages.

Getting out of this swamp illustrates a crucial element in a piece of growth: a person grows more often by means of let-

ting something go than by taking something in. Growth usually *looks* as though it is a matter of taking something in, that
is, "Hey, now he has a new idea, feeling, or perception he
didn't have before—he's grown." But in most cases, the new
element was already there waiting. We are usually faced all
day with material and data which would enable us to grow at
least two or three steps. If we get a "new" idea, or perception,
almost invariably it's the third or seventeenth time we've en-
countered it. This time it *took*. This time growth occurred.
What is really *new* is the letting go of an old perception,
thought, or feeling which was really preventing assimilation of
the "new" thing already waiting in the wings. Thus the crucial
event in growing is often the beginning of a relinquishing:
seeing the shabby side of an old idea or perception for the
first time, seeing around it to its limits, seeing it in perspective, seeing it as a subsidiary of something else—and thus letting go a bit. Only this permits the restructuring necessary for
taking in the new perception, idea, or feeling.

Here is where writing things down can accelerate growth.
When you write things down—as long as you don't write them
down with too much commitment—you are able to see them
in perspective. It is as though holding onto that thought or
perception were a burden for your mind. Writing is a setting
down of that burden and it lets the mind take a rest from it.
Now the mind can better see what is limited about it and
take up a new thought or perception.

The main thing about a perception or thought that prevents
growth is that you don't see it, you only see "through" it like
a lens. It's not so much a thought as a way of thinking. You
can see most of the thoughts you think or sights you see. But
it's hard to see the *way* you think and see. But if you will get
yourself to write freely and uncarefully you have a much bet-

ter chance of seeing these thoughts or perceptions that prevent growth.

In your effort to become sensitive to how writing develops through stages, try to feel how it operates on different time scales. I have been speaking of a short time scale and saying you must accept bad writing in order to end up with something better at the end of four hours or four days; that if you don't, you freeze the development of your words at a premature stage.

But you must develop a feel for the larger growth cycles too. Certain kinds of growth take longer. One has to be open and accept bad writing now—meaning *this year, this decade*—in order to get to good writing. I can now see that a lot of my stuck situations in writing come from trying to write something that I won't be able to write for another ten years: trying to avoid the voice and self I now have.

3

The Process of Writing— Cooking

GROWING is the overall larger process, the evolution of whole organisms. Cooking is the smaller process: bubbling, percolating, fermenting, chemical interaction, atomic fission. Cooking drives the engine that makes growing happen. It's because of cooking that a piece of writing can start out X and end up Y, that a writer can start out after supper seeing, feeling, and knowing one set of things and end up at midnight seeing, feeling, and knowing things he hadn't thought of before. Cooking is the smallest unit of generative action, the smallest piece of anti-entropy whereby a person spends his energy to buy new perceptions and insights from himself.

At first I thought that writing freely was the secret of cooking. If someone who has always written in a controlled way takes off the editorial lid, he tends to produce a burst of cooking. Yet often this is not enough in itself to produce cooking. Sometimes it just makes a barren mess.

Then I thought the heart of cooking was energy. It's true that it takes energy to cook. And sometimes a big burst of energy seems to be what makes cooking happen. But as everyone knows who has tried to write, sometimes no amount of energy suffices to get something written.

I think I've finally figured it out. Cooking is the interaction of contrasting or conflicting material. I try in what follows to specify various *kinds* of interaction that are important in writing. But in any of them cooking consists of the process of one piece of material (or one process) being transformed by interacting with another: one piece of material being seen through the lens of another, being dragged through the guts of another, being reoriented or reorganized in terms of the other, being mapped onto the other.

COOKING AS INTERACTION BETWEEN PEOPLE

The original, commonest, easiest-to-produce kind of interaction is that between people. If you are stuck writing or trying to figure something out, there is nothing better than finding one person, or more, to talk to. If they don't agree or have trouble understanding, so much the better—so long as their minds are not closed. This explains what happens to me and many others countless times: I write a paper; it's not very good; I discuss it with someone; after fifteen minutes of back-and-forth I say something in response to a question or argument of his and he says, "But why didn't you *say* that? That's good. That's clear." I want to shout, "But I *did* say that. The whole paper is saying that." But in truth the whole paper is merely implying or leading up to or circumnavigating that. Until I could see my words and thoughts refracted through his consciousness, I *couldn't* say it directly that way.

Two heads are better than one because two heads can make conflicting material interact better than one head usually can. It's why brain-storming works. I say something. You give a response and it constitutes some restructuring or reorienting of what I said. Then *I* see something new on the basis of your restructuring and so I, in turn, can restructure what I first said. The process provides a continual leverage or mechanical advantage: we each successively climb upon the shoulders of the other's restructuring, so that at each climbing up, we can see a little farther. This is the process by which a discussion or argument "gets somewhere"—and it shows clearly why some discussions get nowhere. When people are stubborn and narrow-minded, they refuse to allow the material in their head to be restructured by what the other person says: they simply hang on to the orientations they have and are too afraid to relinquish any of them.

COOKING AS INTERACTION BETWEEN IDEAS

Just as two people, if they let their ideas interact, can produce ideas or points of view that neither could singly have produced, a lone person, if he learns to maximize the interaction among his own ideas or points of view, can produce new ones that didn't seem available to him.

The way to do this is to encourage conflicts or contradictions in your thinking. We are usually taught to avoid them; and we cooperate in this teaching because it is confusing or frustrating to hold two conflicting ideas at the same time. It feels like a dead end or a trap but really it is the most fruitful situation to be in. Unless you can get yourself into a contradiction, you may be stuck with no power to have any thoughts other than the ones you are already thinking.

It turns out that in your normal round of thinking and perceiving—especially if you are trying to write—you drift into conflicts and contradictions all the time. If you don't seem to, it merely means you have trained yourself not to see them. Follow streams of thought, metaphors and associations better —drift better—and look for disagreements rather than agreements.

One easy way to produce contrasting and conflicting ideas is just to write along, as in a ten-minute exercise, and let yourself drift in different directions. Even if you are sticking more or less to the same material, what you are writing will shift its organizing principle. Look at all your material in terms of one idea or organizing principle and then in terms of the other. Don't worry about the contradictions.

COOKING AS INTERACTION BETWEEN WORDS AND IDEAS, BETWEEN IMMERSION AND PERSPECTIVE

I've spent a lot of time in a debate with myself about whether it's better to work things out in the medium of words or in the medium of ideas and meanings.

When I first discovered the virtues of writing a lot I thought I had discovered that it was always a bad thing to work at the idea level, to make outlines, or to work in terms of "points" or meanings. And that it was always better just to keep on writing at the word level. I clung to this idea for a long time. Even in the face of huge word-swamps I got into and could scarcely get out of. "I haven't written things out in words *enough*," I said to myself. But finally I had to admit to myself that working in thoughts could be a good thing. Here is a diary entry from a time when this lesson was being driven home to me:

I'm stuck with a bad article. I'm trying to rewrite it and can't. It doesn't work; and I can't get anyone to publish it; I finally have to admit that I can feel something weak and wrong or fishy about it. But I can't seem to improve it. Finally a breakthrough from translating my *words* into *thoughts*—forcing myself to restate in *simple brief* form the thoughts that exist in the thing—usually by paragraph: find plus-or-minus one thought in each paragraph. But only genuine thoughts. Be tough about admitting there's no thought in some paragraphs.

It's remarkably liberating. I realize I'd been hypnotized by the words, phrases and sentences I'd worked out with such pain—and I really like them and value them.

And so I came to decide they were both good, but for different purposes: perspective and immersion. Working in ideas gives you perspective, structure, and clarity; working in words gives you fecundity, novelty, richness. Two passages from one entry:

I was hung up in words, enmeshed in them and not seeing around them or with perspective. I cured it by getting *out from under* words and saying "but what *idea* is this really asserting?" . . . What is bad about this process of being mired up in the mess of words is what is good about it: when you are writing along, riding on the rhythms of speech and the energies of syntax, you often wander off the track. Even if you are writing from an outline, you still wander off the track. But this is precisely the process by which I come up with new ideas I could never have known to put in an outline.

But even that view of the two processes didn't always hold true. One day I was forced to notice that sometimes word-writing leads you to just the summing-up you were looking for and couldn't get by trying to "sum-up." And sometimes idea-thinking produces fecundity by giving you a new angle where writing-out was keeping you stuck in one potato patch.

It wasn't till I figured out cooking as interaction that I

could finally understand the relationship between working in words and working in ideas: it's not that one is better than the other; not even that each has a different function. It's the interaction between the two that yields both clarity and richness—cooking. Start with whichever you prefer. But make sure you use both and move back and forth between them. For when you sum up a long set of words into a single thought (even if you do it badly), you always find new things in the words: new implications, relationships, and places where they don't make sense. And when you take a single thought and turn it into a full set of words—put it into someone's mouth —you also find things in that thought you hadn't seen before. Each time you switch modes, you get a new view and more leverage.

COOKING AS INTERACTION
BETWEEN METAPHORS

Interaction between metaphors is interaction of the most fine-grained, generative sort. Make as many metaphors as you can. And analogies, comparisons, examples. Encourage them. Let them roll off your pencil freely. Too much. They produce interaction and cooking just as in the interaction between people or ideas. When you make a metaphor, you call something by a wrong name. If you make a comparison, an analogy, or an example, you are thinking of something in terms of something else. There is always a contradiction. You are not just calling a house a house, but rather a playground, a jungle, a curse, a wound, a paradise. Each throws into relief aspects of the house you might otherwise miss. You are seeing one thought or perception through the lens of another. Here again is the essence of cooking. As in all cooking, new ideas and perceptions result. Connections are loosened so that something may develop or grow in whatever its potential directions are.

Don't make the mistake of thinking you are a "literal-minded person" who doesn't make metaphors: such people don't exist. It is well demonstrated that everyone dreams, and dreams are nothing but metaphors, comparisons, analogies, and examples. If you find it hard to use them, it merely means you are out of the habit of listening to them. Make the ones you can and keep trying to hold your mind open to register the others that are there.

Perhaps you've listened too much to warnings of mixed metaphors. A mixed metaphor is never bad because it's mixed, only because it's badly mixed. (This is only a consideration for final drafts: for earlier drafts, the more "bad" mixing, the better.) Anyone who is against mixed metaphors because they are mixed is like someone who is against kissing twice: he probably doesn't really like kissing once. He's entitled to his taste but he mustn't be taken as a judge of kisses.

COOKING AS INTERACTION BETWEEN MODES

Try to encourage the same thing with different modes or textures of writing. Allow your writing to fall into poetry and then back into prose; from informal to formal; from personal to impersonal; first-person to third-person; fiction, nonfiction; empirical, *a priori*. When it starts to change modes on you, don't shrink back and stop it. Let it go and develop itself in that mode. Even if it seems crazy. It will show you things about your material and help it to cook, develop, and grow.

First you are writing about a dog you had; then you are writing about sadness; then you are writing about personalities of dogs; then about the effect of the past; then a poem about names; then an autobiographical self-analysis; then a story about your family. Each way of writing will bring out different aspects of the material.

COOKING AS INTERACTION BETWEEN YOU AND SYMBOLS ON PAPER

Language is the principal medium that allows you to interact with yourself. (Painters do it with shapes and colors, composers with musical sounds.) Without a symbol system such as language, it is difficult if not impossible to think about more than one thing at a time, and thus to allow two thoughts to interact and cook. Putting a thought into symbols means setting it down and letting the mind take a rest from it. With language you can put an idea or feeling or perception into words—put it in your cud or put it in the freezer—and then go on to have a different one and not lose the first. In this way, you can entertain two thoughts or feelings at the same time or think about the relationship between two thoughts or feelings. A principle value of language, therefore, is that it permits you to *distance* yourself from your own perceptions, feelings, and thoughts.

Try, then, to write words on paper so as to permit an interaction between you and not-you. You are building someone to talk to. This means two stages: first put out words on paper as freely as possible, trying to be so fully involved that you don't even think about it and don't experience any gap between you and the words: just talk onto the paper. But then, in the second stage, stand back and make as large a gap as you can between you and the words: set them aside and then pick them up and try to read them as though they came out of someone else. Learn to interact with them, react to them. Learn to let them produce a new reaction or response in you.

One of the functions of a diary is to create interaction between you and symbols on paper. If you have strong feelings and then write them down freely, it gives you on the one hand some distance and control, but on the other hand it often makes you feel those feelings *more*. For you can often allow yourself to feel something more if you are not so helpless and lost in the middle of it. So the writing helps you feel the feeling and then go on to feel the next feelings. Not be stuck.

NONCOOKING

You can help cooking happen by making it more overt. For this it helps to understand why cooking sometimes doesn't happen.

There are two kinds of noncooking. The first is when there aren't any contrasting or conflicting elements to interact. This is the situation when you know what you have to say, you say it, and it is perfectly straightforward. If you already have brilliant fully-cooked material lying around in your head, you are fine. But usually what you have isn't very interesting, satisfactory, or sufficient. You need better material, you need some good ideas, you need some good things to say. This can usually be cured by writing a lot, lifting the editorial lid, babbling or doing ten-minute exercises.

The first kind of noncooking is illustrated by a group of people who all agree with each other. No one can do anything but nod his head or else say, "And here's another reason I agree with you." Sometimes you have the same effect when everyone is excessively "nice" and there is nothing but agreement in the room: no energy, no ideas, no different perceptions.

But there is a different kind of noncooking where there is plenty of conflicting material but it won't interact. This kind of noncooking can also be vividly illustrated by a group of people. This time the group is full of disagreement, but whenever someone starts to say something, he is immediately interrupted by someone else starting to say why he disagrees with what (he thinks) the person was starting to say. There is no fruitful interaction, there is none of the productive phenomenon of one idea or perception refracted or seen through the lens of another. There is only deadlock and stalemate. Two strong men arm-wrestling: great energy expended, muscles bulging, sweat popping out on the foreheads, but no movement.

I warm to this second sort of noncooking: being caught in irons between a lot of contrasting material but being unable to cook it. Instead of interacting, the material just locks horns. You start to follow one idea or train of thought or way of writing but then you see it's no good; then another, but you see it, too, doesn't work; then another and the same thing. You try the first one again, but don't get any farther. Frustration.

The problem of the argumentative group illustrates how to get cooking going. They need to stop all the interrupting and make sure each speaker finishes what he is saying before someone else speaks. In this way they can maximize the chance of one person's view actually getting inside the head of the other people and being transmuted or reoriented there.

So, too, if you are stuck because your ideas won't interact.

Take each idea singly. Pretend to espouse each one whole-heartedly. See everything in terms of it. Pretend you are a person who is convinced of it. This amounts to giving each idea a full hearing and insures that the interaction happens—that the other material is seen through its lens.

You get a similar kind of noncooking when there is no interaction between writing-out and summing-up—working in words and working in meanings. You start writing but before you get very far you stop writing because you sense something wrong. This happens again and again. I can only break out of this sort of noncooking—which is perhaps my major stuckpoint—if I quite consciously force myself to make the interaction overt in two painfully separated steps. This means that if I am writing I must consciously prevent myself from switching to the sitting-back-wondering-whether-it-makes-sense cycle. If I see it doesn't make sense I must keep writing —perhaps about *why* it doesn't make sense or if possible start saying things that do make sense. But not stop.

Only after a full cycle of writing—ten or twenty minutes at least—can I let myself stand back and think in perspective. And when I start this contrasting mode, I must also force myself to keep at it till it too completes its cycle. For example, I would *not* have brought the perspective cycle to completion if I simply ended up with "Causes of the French Revolution" or "Things I felt Monday afternoon when I walked along the river" or "Contrasts between this candidate and that candidate." None of those phrases has a verb. None says anything, asserts anything. I haven't yet finished sitting back and thinking what things add up to.

If you want to insure cooking you have to make more than one interaction: if you start with words, it's not good enough just to translate into assertions; it's the movement

from immersion to perspective and *then back to immersion*—
or vice versa—that really strengthens and refines what you are
producing. And the more transitions, the more strengthening,
the more refining.

A stuckpoint:

All these ideas rolling around in my head about motives for teaching and reasons why my plan is good. I can find words for them
separately but I am going crazy spending tons of time, because I
can't write them down—can't figure out where to begin. It's like a
tangled ball of string and I can't find the end. I can only find
loops. If I were in a conversation or argument, I would express
all these points—I could bring them out when they were needed
in response to the words of the other person. But here I've got no
other person. I feel like I'm in a terrible vacuum, in a sensory-
deprivation room, trying to fight my way out of a wet paper bag
when there are endless folds of wet paper and though I fight
through each fold, there's still more soggy, dank, sodden, smelly
paper hanging all over me.

Here was a situation where I let myself remain stuck at the
same intermediate distance from my words: I allowed myself
to remain halfway between dealing with my words as me and
as not-me, instead of forcing an interaction between the two
modes. I needed to get closer—write faster and make the words
merely me; and then move back and treat them as not-me. By
building someone to argue with, I would have managed to get
all my ideas into words. Admittedly, they would have been a
great mess—as in an argument—but eventually I would have
seen some workable shape for what I was trying to say and
finally would have found somewhere to start. (Or—if you
want to see this as a problem in starting—I couldn't find a
place to *start* until I started anywhere and wrote a great deal
first.)

If you are having difficulty with a poem or story perhaps it is a problem of noncooking. Perhaps you are not letting it go all the way toward being sad or happy or expressing some particular theme, because you feel that would be going too far: you don't want it to be that extreme. But you may not be able to cook it unless you allow each of the elements or themes or impulses to have its day. Let it go through two or three conflicting versions, or let it be grossly inconsistent from part to part. That's the way to maximize the interaction that will finally cook it down to what you want.

Out of this strategy for dealing with noncooking we can see a more universal piece of advice for all cooking and growing. Almost always it is good to use extremes and let moderation arrive eventually. Being in the middle is being stuck, barren, held between opposites. When there are cycles to be gone through, do each one to the extreme—keep yourself from being caught in the middle. You can't be a good, ruthless editor unless you are a messy, rich producer. But you can't be really fecund as a producer unless you know you'll be able to go at it with a ruthless knife.

DESPERATION WRITING

I know I am not alone in my recurring twinges of panic that I won't be able to write something when I need to, I won't be able to produce coherent speech or thought. And that lingering doubt is a great hindrance to writing. It's a constant fog or static that clouds the mind. I never got out of its clutches till I discovered that it was possible to write something—not something great or pleasing but at least something usable, workable—when my mind is out of commission. The trick is that you have to do all your cooking out on the table:

your mind is incapable of doing any inside. It means using symbols and pieces of paper not as a crutch but as a wheel chair.

The first thing is to admit your condition: because of some mood or event or whatever, your mind is incapable of anything that could be called thought. It can put out a babbling kind of speech utterance, it can put a simple feeling, perception, or sort-of-thought into understandable (though terrible) words. But it is incapable of considering anything in relation to anything else. The moment you try to hold that thought or feeling up against some other to see the relationship, you simply lose the picture—you get nothing but buzzing lines or waving colors.

So admit this. Avoid anything more than one feeling, perception, or thought. Simply write as much as possible. Try simply to steer your mind in the direction or general vicinity of the thing you are trying to write about and start writing and keep writing.

Just write and keep writing. (Probably best to write on only one side of the paper in case you should want to cut parts out with scissors—but you probably won't.) Just write and keep writing. It will probably come in waves. After a flurry, stop and take a brief rest. But don't stop too long. Don't think about what you are writing or what you have written or else you will overload the circuit again. Keep writing as though you are drugged or drunk. Keep doing this till you feel you have a lot of material that might be useful; or, if necessary, till you can't stand it any more—even if you doubt that there's anything useful there.

Then take a pad of little pieces of paper—or perhaps 3x5 cards—and simply start at the beginning of what you were writing, and as you read over what you wrote, every time you

come to any thought, feeling, perception, or image that could
be gathered up into one sentence or one assertion, do so and
write it by itself on a little sheet of paper. In short, you are trying to turn, say, ten or twenty pages of wandering mush into
twenty or thirty hard little crab apples. Sometimes there won't
be many on a page. But if it seems to you that there are none
on a page, you are making a serious error—the same serious
error that put you in this comatose state to start with. You are
mistaking lousy, stupid, second-rate, wrong, childish, foolish,
worthless ideas for no ideas at all. Your job is not to pick out
good ideas but to pick out ideas. As long as you were conscious, your words will be full of things that could be called
feelings, utterances, ideas—things that can be squeezed into
one simple sentence. This is your job. Don't ask for too much.

After you have done this, take those little slips or cards,
read through them a number of times—not struggling with
them, simply wandering and mulling through them; perhaps
shifting them around and looking through them in various
sequences. In a sense these are cards you are playing solitaire
with, and the rules of this particular game permit shuffling
the unused pile.

The goal of this procedure with the cards is to get them to
distribute themselves in two or three or ten or fifteen different piles on your desk. You can get them to do this almost by
themselves if you simply keep reading through them in different orders; certain cards will begin to feel like they go with
other cards. I emphasize this passive, thoughtless mode because I want to talk about desperation writing in its pure
state. In practice, almost invariably at some point in the procedure, your sanity begins to return. It is often at this point.
You actually are moved to have thoughts or—and the difference between active and passive is crucial here—to *exert*

thought: to hold two cards together and *build* or *assert* a relationship. It is a matter of bringing energy to bear.

So you may start to be able to do something active with these cards, and begin actually to think. But if not, just allow the cards to find their own piles with each other by feel, by drift, by intuition, by mindlessness.

You have now engaged in the two main activities that will permit you to get something cooked out on the table rather than in your brain: writing out into messy words, summing up into single assertions, and even sensing relationships between assertions. You can simply continue to deploy these two activities.

If, for example, after that first round of writing, assertion-making, and pile-making, your piles feel as though they are useful and satisfactory for what you are writing—paragraphs or sections or trains of thought—then you can carry on from there. See if you can gather each pile up into a single assertion. When you can, then put the subsidiary assertions of that pile into their best order to fit with that single unifying one. If you *can't* get the pile into one assertion, then take the pile as the basis for doing some more writing out into words. In the course of this writing, you may produce for yourself the single unifying assertion you were looking for; or you may have to go through the cycle of turning the writing into assertions and piles and so forth. Perhaps more than once. The pile may turn out to want to be two or more piles itself; or it may want to become part of a pile you already have. This is natural. This kind of meshing into one configuration, then coming apart, then coming together and meshing into a different configuration—this is growing and cooking. It makes a terrible mess, but if you can't do it in your head, you have to put up with a cluttered desk and a lot of confusion.

If, on the other hand, all that writing *didn't* have useful material in it, it means that your writing wasn't loose, drifting, quirky, jerky, associative enough. This time try especially to let things simply remind you of things that are seemingly crazy or unrelated. Follow these odd associations. Make as many metaphors as you can—be as nutty as possible—and explore the metaphors themselves—open them out. You may have all your energy tied up in some area of your experience that you are leaving out. Don't refrain from writing about whatever else is on your mind: how you feel at the moment, what you are losing your mind over, randomness that intrudes itself on your consciousness, the pattern on the wallpaper, what those people you see out the window have on their minds—though keep coming back to the whateveritis you are supposed to be writing about. Treat it, in short, like ten-minute writing exercises. Your best perceptions and thoughts are always going to be tied up in whatever is really occupying you, and that is also where your energy is. You may end up writing a love poem—or a hate poem—in one of those little piles while the other piles will finally turn into a lab report on data processing or whatever you have to write about. But you couldn't, in your present state of having your head shot off, have written that report without also writing the poem. And the report will have some of the juice of the poem in it and vice versa.

THE GOAL IS COOKING

Desperation writing seemed magic. As though I had found secret powers and was getting something for nothing: new ideas where formerly I was barren; structure where formerly I remained stuck in chaos. Gradually I began to fear there must be some catch—I would be punished for violating nature, my own powers would be cut off:

It's scary. I think I'm developing a dependency on this prosthesis for the mind. My mind is turning to slush. I can no longer seem to hold three ideas in my mouth at the same time like I used to. I'm always resorting to prosthesis. And I can't seem to make myself write well any more. I just write flabby, mushy, soupy. No backbone in my head. I'll go blind and insane if I indulge myself in this easiness—if I continue to use this crutch, my organs will dry up and atrophy.

Is it really true? I think I'm able to do more complicated things now——work at a higher level—but is this wishful thinking to disguise the fact that I'm writing badly and slowly and something seems screwed up about my attempts to write this book?

As far as I can tell I still have all my powers. But I was right to sense something was fishy. It is possible to abuse this approach and I was tending to do so. The mistake hinged on failing to distinguish between *cooking* and *external cooking*. Since external cooking got me out my bind, I mistook it for the goal. Finally I began to distinguish the two.

I may be falling in love with the process, the externalizing of the organic process outside the organism. But it's only the means to an end: cooking. If you're not cooking, externalize it to make it happen; but once you get yourself cooking, don't make the mistake of thinking that it's better to have it external; the truth is that it's better to have it *internal:* things cook at a hotter temperature and you get a more permanent, magical, fine-grained, extensive transmutation of elements than you could ever get externally.

The extreme of external cooking is "desperation writing," which I have just described. The extreme of internal cooking is what I call "magic writing": cooking which is wholly internal, hidden, and sometimes instantaneous. I think of Mozart writing out a completed symphony as fast as he could write; or A. E. Housman ending up with a perfectly polished poem after a lunch of beer and a sleepy walk in the sun.

External cooking is like mixing up dry ingredients in a bowl, whereas internal cooking is like dissolving them in water so they integrate at the molecular level. Internal cooking produces more force and voice in the words: this integrated texture is more clear and powerful; every cell of the final product contains a plan or microcosm (gene) of the whole. This is why freewriting can produce writing that is better than most slow careful writing.

Also, internal cooking is in fact quicker and takes less energy. External cooking is like low gear on a bicycle. When you first discover low gear, it seems as though you are getting something for nothing: you now easily conquer a hill you couldn't get up before. But in actual fact, if you had been able to *stay* in high gear, you would have gotten up the hill with less energy. It was wasteful to take all those strokes in that lower gear. But you would have had to be *much* stronger to save this energy. (Only the rich can afford to economize.) Similarly, internal cooking means getting the whole pot boiling at once and having it go through changes as a whole. Whereas external cooking means taking it into separate little pots and cooking each one with less fuel—but the total fuel bill is greater. You save energy if you cook the whole thing at once—and spill less, too—but you need a bigger burst of energy or strength. And you need to endure a hotter temperature.

Moral: use external cooking when you need it. Be good at using it. Use it especially to get cooking going. But don't think you can use it to beat the system and avoid cooking. If you want to write, you must cook. There is always a *crunch* in writing. The crunch feels to me like lifting the Empire State building; like folding up a ten-acre parachute on a windy field. You can't avoid the crunch. It takes heat, electricity, acid to cook. If you can't stand the heat, get out of the kitchen. If you don't like the excitement or energy that is building up in your guts, your head, your forearms, it is possible to abuse external cooking and use it to dissipate this heat, acid, electricity.

The important thing, then, is not these specific practices I have described which are usually ways to produce external cooking. Cooking is the goal. Concentrate on trying to get a feel for cooking—for words and ideas interacting into a higher, more organized state. Govern your behavior according to the principle that whatever makes it happen is right for you and whatever gets in its way is wrong.

But I would stress that for most people—that majority of people who have trouble writing—external cooking usually increases cooking. It gets you cooking at last. It sets higher but reachable standards for you: you insist on cooking whatever you write. If you get to the point where you are abusing it— where you are cooking too many things in thimbles with matches when you could actually throw it all into a pressure cooker and put the heat on high—you will know it and move in that direction.

COOKING AND ENERGY

This model helps you understand the relationship of energy or exertion to writing. It takes energy to make material end up more organized than it started—to go against the grain of things or swim upstream. But it also takes energy to sit around trying to cook and not succeed. It is important to begin to get the feel for different kinds of energy expenditure in your writing so you can grow wiser about when you are wasting your time.

—There is the energy of being stuck: trying to cook when you can't. Perhaps you are at the early stage where you can't find words at all; or later when there are many words and much material, but you are stuck and unable to bring any shape or coherence to them. This is wasted energy. Get cooking going.

—The energy of trying to make a lousy first draft good: trying to avoid cooking. You are not willing to put out energy, to build up the heat. You might as well get up and stop writing till you are willing.

—The energy of internal or magic cooking. It is somewhat mysterious but you are sitting on heat or acid and it is working on the material. You are writing and it is coming out well. Or you are not writing—sitting or walking around—but you can feel it bubbling inside. Things are going well. You can feel it's not wasted energy even if you are not writing.

—The energy of external cooking. Getting yourself to write a lot. Whenever you bog down, getting yourself either to start writing things out or summing them up. Using lots of paper. Producing a lot you know isn't good which you know you will have to throw away. It's inefficient compared to perfect internal cooking. But it's very efficient compared to not cooking. And you can make it lead to internal cooking.

Many people have what is almost an inverse relationship between energy and results. A writing session either "goes well" or it doesn't: either they write something relatively quickly and relatively easily and it comes out well; or else it's no good, and it gets no better no matter how hard they work on it. What this means is that they can cook *only* internally, otherwise they are stuck. But if you can feel better how energy relates to various kinds of cooking, you can avoid this situation, make writing less mysterious, and make your results more proportional to the energy you put in.

ADVERTISEMENT: I used to find writing exhausting. Then I figured out how to grow and cook it. I still find writing exhausting. But now I write more and better and even finish things.

GOODNESS AND BADNESS

Some readers feel I am asking them to write as badly as possible. I am not. Your goal is good writing. The mind is magic. It can cook things instantaneously and perfectly when it gets going. You should expect yourself at times to write straight onto the paper words and thoughts far better than you knew were in you. You should look for it and want it. To expect anything less is to consider yourself brain-damaged.

But a person's best writing is often all mixed up together with his worst. It all feels lousy to him as he's writing, but if he will let himself write it and come back later he will find some parts of it are excellent. It is as though one's best words come wrapped in one's worst. For most people, some of their strongest sounds, rhythms, and textures—and some of their best insights—only occur when they stop censoring and write carelessly. Yet when they stop censoring, of course, they will produce some of their worst.

We all tend to believe in word-magic: if I think words, my mind will be tricked into believing them; if I speak those words, I'll believe them more strongly; and if I actually write them down, I am somehow secretly committed to them and my behavior is determined by them. It is crucial to learn to write words and not believe them or feel hypnotized at all. It can even be good practice to write as badly or as foolishly as you can. If you can't write anything at all, it is probably because you are too squeamish to let yourself write badly.

WHY THE OLD, WRONG MODEL OF
WRITING PERSISTS

If the picture I am giving of the writing process is correct and the one I am fighting is wrong, this fact itself needs explaining. Is it possible that people can persist for such a long time believing that you reach up to touch the floor? There are various reasons.

For one thing, the old two-step model—the meaning-into-words model—is not really wrong, it's simply not complete. For in almost any piece of writing, the last stage of the growth process—the mopping up or editorial stage—is just what the old model describes: get your meaning straight and then find the best words. Of all the steps in the growth cycle, this one is the most obvious because it is the most conscious and manipulative. Thus people easily mistake it for the writing process itself.

For another thing, instead of recognizing cooking and growing as a coherent process, most people simply experience them as some kind of *absence* of coherent process: as inspiration, as a lucky mess, or as a disaster. When you start out try-

ing to write X and it comes out Y—and it happens quickly and
you like Y—you are apt to call it inspiration. We call it inspiration and feel an external source of enlightenment because it is an extreme case of the words, thoughts, and images
cooking and growing according to their own plan. People try
to heighten inspiration by procedures which inhibit the conscious, manipulative, and planning parts of the self (that is,
by taking drugs, being drunk, or writing while half-asleep).

When you start out trying to write X and it comes out Y—
and you like Y, but it took a long, chaotic, wandering,
swampy path to get there—you tend to call it a lucky mess.
You say to yourself, "Isn't it amazing that I came up with
something good when I'm so disorganized and careless. I
didn't follow my outline at all. (Or I'm so sloppy I didn't even
make an outline.) I guess I'm naturally unfitted for writing.
Next time I better be careful and write the way you're supposed to."

The most frequent result of cooking and growing, however,
is that they are mistaken for disaster and stamped out. On the
level of the sentence, it is the familiar case of a sentence starting out one way, slipping in the middle, and starting to come
out different. Familiar enough: cross it out, wrench it back
into line. At the level of a whole piece or section, you are
writing X, you are well along the way, you have struggled
hard to figure out what you are trying to say, and struggled
hard to make all those sentences say it. And now you are in
the middle of some sentence which suddenly starts to imply
Y. What's worse is that this sentence makes you suspect it is
right and X is wrong! But you've invested so much in all
those sentences. You either call yourself an idiot and rip it up
in disgust and go to bed saying the hell with it. Or else, since
you need the piece tomorrow, you try to pretend you didn't

hear that sentence whispering Y. You try to tuck everything
Y under the rug and hope the reader won't notice.

And so, because cooking and growing are not recognized as
good when they *do* occur, they don't occur enough. Millions
of people simply don't write: they find it too frustrating or
unrewarding simply because they cannot make cooking
happen. Also there are many people who succeed in following the old model. They patch up, mop up, neaten up the
half-cooked and unsatisfactory ideas they find lying around in
their head. What they write is boring and obvious. Schools
often reward boring obvious writing. Then there are the tiny
minority of cases in which someone finds already lying around
in his head something brilliant and interesting. And so he too
can write according to the old model.

One other reason for the persistence of the old model: it
promises structure and control and that's just what you yearn
for when you're having trouble with writing.

CONCLUSION

If you have a way of writing that works well for you, keep it
(and teach it to others). But if you have difficulty with writing,
try this model and try to understand your difficulty as a problem in cooking or growing.

Make writing a global task, not a piecemeal one. All parts
of a piece of writing are interdependent. No part is done till
all parts are done. If you think there are four sections in what
you have to write, the worst thing you can do is write them
separately so you finish one before going on to the next. This
prevents interaction, cooking, growing. Make yourself sketch
in all four parts quickly and lightly; then work some more on

each part, letting it go where it needs to; continue improving all the parts; and only finish one part when you are also ready to finish the others. The thing may grow into five parts or two parts (and it's got to grow, also, into a unity). Or even if it stays in four parts, your working out of part four is necessary before you can really work out the first part right.

You don't have to give up the satisfaction that comes from getting a task partly done. But change the model: get that satisfaction from finishing a run-through of the *whole thing*, not finishing the first section.

If this long story of writing-as-growing-and-cooking seems complicated, there are really only two main points:

1. Cooking means getting material to interact. The interaction that is most important to me is the interaction between writing out and summing up (working in words and working in meanings). If you are having trouble with your writing, try to increase the interaction of these two processes. Avoid doing all writing or doing all sitting-back-thinking. And above all avoid being caught in the middle where you write only a couple of sentences and stop and wonder and worry. Make each cycle complete: at least ten minutes of involved writing; then stop completely to see what it all adds up to or is trying to add up to.

2. Growing means getting words to evolve through stages. The growing stage I find most important is writing a lot. If you can get yourself writing a lot, this will spur the other growing processes (encouraging chaos, finding a center of gravity, and editing). Here are some concrete suggestions if you have difficulty writing a lot:

   a) Simply stop and do a strict ten-minute writing exercise. Because these exercises are governed by rigid rules, last only ten minutes, and ask you to write absolutely anything, they make it easier for you to deal with whatever static in your head is tying your tongue.

b) Talk to yourself in your writing. If you stop involuntarily in the middle of a sentence when you suddenly see it's turning out stupid or wrong, force yourself to keep writing and write to yourself whatever it is you have to say about that sentence: why it is stupid or wrong, how you noticed it, whatever. This activity helps more than any other to keep me from bogging down. It frees my voice and my writing. It breaks down the barrier that says I keep my real words to myself and only write "prepared" words for my audience.

c) Don't let beginnings be a problem. Write through them by brute force. I often have to use all-purpose beginnings: "And another thing . . ."; "The thing of it is . . ."; "What I want to talk about is . . ."; "You want to know something?" At the end you can write better beginnings.

d) If you are stuck badly, pretend you are with a person or an audience and you only have a half-hour to tell them what you have to say. Of course you *should* have it perfectly prepared, but since you don't, you've simply got to start somewhere, anywhere, and keep writing, hemming and hawing, getting it out somehow. You may have to force yourself by using a watch and really only giving yourself that half-hour. It's the sort of process in which after you've been going for fifteen or twenty minutes it often happens that you write, "Yes, now I see what it is that I'm trying to tell you; now I see the point of all this." This is just what you are trying to make happen, but it won't happen unless you plunge in and just write.

e) If you are even more stuck and you think that the act of writing itself is causing more static than is worth fighting, you can do the same thing talking. But you must be strict or it doesn't work. You must set out the clock, talk *out loud,* and keep talking as though there were someone listening and no place to hide.

f) If, no matter what you try, you still can't write, then don't call it writing. Get up and do something else. Don't sit down with pencil and paper till you are prepared to write. A part of you is refusing to write, and if that part of you is so strong that it is calling the shots, you had better start listening to it. Find out why it refuses. That "it" is you.

4

The Teacherless Writing Class

I HAVE been speaking till now as though writing were a transaction entirely with yourself. It *is* a transaction with yourself—lonely and frustrating—and I have wanted, in fact, to increase that transaction: help you do *more* business with yourself. But writing is also a transaction with other people. Writing is not just getting things down on paper, it is getting things inside someone else's head. If you wish to improve your writing you must also learn to do more business with other people. That is the goal of the teacherless writing class.

Imagine you are blind and deaf. You want to speak better. But you are in perpetual darkness and silence. You send out words as best you can but no words come back. You get a few clues about your speaking: perhaps you asked for something and didn't get it; or you got the wrong thing. You know you did something wrong. What you aren't getting is the main thing that helps people speak better: direct feedback to your speech—a directly perceived sense of how different people react to the sounds you make.

This is an image of what it is like when you try to improve your writing all by yourself. You simply don't know what your words make happen in readers. Perhaps you are even taking a writing course and a teacher tells you what he thinks the weak and strong points were and suggests things you should try for. But you usually get little sense of what the words actually did to him—how he *perceived* and *experienced* them. Besides, he's only one person and not very typical of other readers either. Writing is a string you send out to connect yourself with other consciousnesses, but usually you never have the opportunity to feel anything at the other end. How can you tell whether you've got a fish if the line always feels slack?

The teacherless writing class tries to remedy this situation. It tries to take you out of darkness and silence. It is a class of seven to twelve people. It meets at least once a week. Everyone reads everyone else's writing. Everyone tries to give each writer a sense of how his words were experienced. The goal is for the writer to come as close as possible to being able to see and experience his own words *through* seven or more people. That's all.

To improve your writing you don't need advice about what changes to make; you don't need theories of what is good and bad writing. You need movies of people's minds while they read your words. But you need this for a sustained period of time—at least two or three months. And you need to get the experience of not just a couple of people but of at least six or seven. And you need to keep getting it from the *same* people so that they get better at transmitting their experience and you get better at hearing them. And you must write something *every* week. Even if you are very busy, even if you have nothing to write about, and even if you are very blocked, you must write something and try to experience it through their eyes. Of course it may not be good; you may not be satisfied with it. But if you only learn how people perceive and experience words you are satisfied with, you are missing a crucial area of learning. You often learn the most from reactions to words that you loathe. Do you want to learn how to write or protect your feelings?

In the following pages I try to help you set up and use a teacherless writing class. If you are ever confused, remember that everything is designed to serve only one utterly simple goal: the writer should learn how his words were *actually* experienced by these particular readers.

SETTING UP THE CLASS

You need a committed group of people

For a successful class you need the same people writing and taking part every week. People need time to get better at giving reactions and hearing them. Learning to make use of a teacherless class is a struggle. It's too easy to avoid the struggle by letting the class peter out. People have to know the others will be there.

The best solution is to have a few trial classes for people to explore the class. Keep having trial classes and bringing in more people until you finally get at least seven people who will make an explicit commitment for the next ten weeks. Don't start the real class till you have those seven. And make sure everyone has explicitly stated his commitment. It's only ten weeks, but that period is crucial.

You may want to restrict the class to the committed, or else invite in others who are not sure they can come consistently. Two warnings, though: avoid more than twelve in one class; and avoid having people there who haven't put in a piece of writing themselves.

What kind of people?

There are obvious advantages to having friends, colleagues, or people who have a lot in common. If all are working on the same kind of writing, this helps everyone understand each other better.

But I always stick up for the advantages of diversity: different kinds of people working on different kinds of writing. It can make some strain. But the feedback is better. The poet needs the experience of the businessman reading his poem just as the businessman needs the experience of the poet reading his committee report. If each thinks the other's writing has no meaning or no value this is an advantage rather than a disadvantage. Each needs to experience what it was like for the other to find the writing worthless, and where the other sees glimmers. A poet needs the experiences of other poets, but if that's all he gets the range of reactions is crucially restricted: poets are liable to react too exclusively in terms of the tradition—how it follows some poems and departs from others. Whenever people work in only one genre, they gradually become blind to certain excrescences.

What to write?

The main thing is that it doesn't matter so long as you write something. Treat the rigid requirement as a blessing. Since you must crank out something every week, expect some of it to be terrible. You can't improve your writing unless you put out words differently from the way you put them out now, and find out how these new kinds of writing are experienced. You can't try out new ways of generating words unless many

of them feel embarrassing, terrible, or frightening. But you
will be surprised in two ways. Some passages you hate you'll
discover to be good. And some of the reactions which most
improve your writing are brought on by terrible writing—
writing you wouldn't have shown to someone if you'd had
more time to rewrite.

Use whatever procedure you think best for deciding what
to write. Write the same kind of thing over and over again—
even the same piece over and over again if you wish. Or try
out wildly different things. There is no best or right way. If
you have the desire to write, there is probably some particular
kind of writing you dream of doing. Do it. Or if there's something different you feel you should work on first, follow your
own advice.

If you continually have trouble thinking of something to
write, you should probably begin to suspect that some part of
you is trying to undermine your efforts at writing. But don't
spend so much time psyching yourself out that you don't get
writing done.

If you are stuck for things to write, here are some suggestions.

Ten-minute writing exercises are probably the best way out of
this problem. See chapter 1.

Put words on paper in order to make something observable
happen. This gives you a down-to-earth, concrete way of deciding
whether the words worked. For example, write a letter asking for
a refund on something; a letter to be published in a newspaper;
something funny enough to make someone actually laugh out
loud; a letter that will get someone to go out on a date with you;
a journal entry that actually takes you out of one mood and puts
you in another. Try to stop thinking about whether the writing
is good or bad, right or wrong: ask whether it *worked* or *didn't
work*.

Hand in writing you need for some other purpose, such as for a course or a job. Use it in class first so you can improve it on the basis of reactions. (Watch out here that they concentrate on telling you how they experienced it and not try to tell you how to fix it. You can decide later how to fix it if they'll give you their perceptions.)

Describe a person, place, or incident that means a lot to you.

Describe such a person, place, or incident but from an unfamiliar angle: for example, describe the place as though you were blind and could only know it through your other senses; describe the person as though you had only met him once or as though it were he describing himself; describe the incident as though it had never happened and you were only imagining it.

Describe something while you are in a definite mood. Or pretend to be in that mood describing it. Or write in a particular mood. Don't mention the mood in the writing and get readers to tell you what mood comes through.

Write something in the voice of someone you know. Don't so much try to think about his voice or the way he speaks or writes: just try to be *in* his head and speak onto the paper. Don't tell readers who it is. Get them to describe the speaker they hear.

Write a conversation or a dialogue between two or three people. Again, try to write from within the voices and get the readers to tell you about the voices they hear.

Write about a character or object in a story, movie, or photograph.

Write an important letter. The classic one is a letter of blame to your own parents. Or a letter of appreciation.

Define something that is important to you but difficult to define. Suggestions: how is it different from things that are similar; what is it a subset or subdivision of; what are subsets or subdivisions of it.

Tell a belief or conviction of yours in such a way as to make the reader believe that you really do believe it. (This is what is involved in applying to a draft board for conscientious objector status.) This is not the same as trying to make *him* believe it.

Describe a belief or develop an argument in order to convince someone who disagrees. Keep in mind that this is often impossible.

Write a poem. Suggestions: find one you like and rewrite it, translate it, or write one just like it; write the poem as it would be if it were about a different topic or expressing a different feeling; write another poem this poet would write; write the poem this poet would write if he were you; write the words or lyrics that go with a piece of music; write a love poem.

Should you hand out copies or read your writing out loud?

There are advantages both ways. Giving out copies saves class time: silent reading is quicker, you can stop and think, go back, read more carefully, and if it is a long piece of writing, people can take it home with them and read it there. This procedure may be more possible than you think. Many photocopying processes are cheap; people can easily write or type onto ditto or mimeo masters; it is often possible for members to leave a single copy of their piece where everyone else can read it carefully before class.

But reading out loud is good too. When you read your writing out loud, you often see things in it that you don't see any other way. Hearing your own words out loud gives you the vicarious experience of being someone else. Reading your words out loud stresses what is most important: writing is really a voice spread out over time, not marks spread out in space. The audience can't experience them all at once as they can a picture; they can only hear one instant at a time as with music. And there must be a voice in it.

Reading out loud also gives you a better idea of the effect of your words on an audience: they cannot go back to try to make sure their reactions are more "careful," "correct," or "objective." For example, someone may say "there were no details" when in fact there were quite a few, or "it doesn't have any organization so I felt lost," when in fact you had a careful structure. But this is good. You need to learn that the details or the structure didn't work for that reader. It's more important to learn what actually got through to a real reader than what might get through to an ideal reader. When a listener misinterprets something which he might have gotten right if he'd had a copy in his hands, his mistake is probably evidence of a real undertow in the writing. That undertow operates even on readers who have the paper in their hands and can read more carefully, but they often don't feel the undertow so they make you pay for it in more mysterious ways: more vague dissatisfactions and misinterpretations.

The nervousness you feel at reading out loud is part of your problem in writing. Even if you don't feel it *as you write,* that only means you've separated your experience of audience from your experience of writing. The fear of the audience is still affecting you somehow: it may be tying your tongue and clouding your mind when you sit down to write; or it may be closing off certain kinds of writing to you. Reading out loud brings the sense of audience back into your act of writing. This is a great source of power. Getting a sense of audience isn't just practice in feeling scared about how they might react. It also means learning how they *do* react. Most people are liberated by finally getting the reactions they fear most— usually extreme criticism or extreme praise. They discover the world doesn't fall apart.

When you read something out loud in class, however, always read it twice and allow at least a minute of silence after each reading for impressions to come clearer in your listeners.

Class time

Find a regular time and stick to it. Otherwise you are asking
for trouble.

As to how much time, fifteen to twenty minutes is sufficient
for seven people to try to tell a writer how each of them perceived and experienced a short piece of writing. This means
a class of eight people should get along with two to two-
and-a-half hours a week. More time may be interesting and
useful if people can spare it. But the essential process in this
sort of class is to get what you can and then move on. You can
never finish giving or getting the experience of a set of words.
Instead of investing more and more minutes on one particular piece of writing, invest more and more weeks so everyone
can begin to get good at this process. Keep the long haul in
mind. Don't let the class take up so much time that people
find it painful to keep coming. Besides, you usually can not
make a significant improvement in your writing in less than
two or three months no matter what kind of learning process
you use. Learning to write is an exercise in slow, underground learning.

A chairman

A chairman or leader can make things run more smoothly,
keep an eye on the clock so that everyone's writing gets its
fair share of time, help people overcome unproductive habits
like talking too much or too little, and generally keep an eye
out. This can make people feel more comfortable.

But it's possible to get along without a chairman too. It
puts more of a burden on everyone, but it can also encourage

everyone to take more responsibility for how the class goes. Whatever your decision, build in a procedure for periodic redecision about whether to have one or who it should be.

Reactions to the class itself

Devote the last five minutes of each class to the class itself as though it were a piece of writing. How do the members perceive and experience that class meeting? The reactions can be communicated by speaking, or you can all do a five-minute freewriting exercise and pass them around. Don't think of this as a time for actually solving dissatisfactions. The same learning principles apply here as to writing: what is valuable is shared perception and experience, not advice about how to fix things. Problems will be solved gradually this way, but better.

GIVING MOVIES OF YOUR MIND

As a reader giving your reactions, keep in mind that you are not answering a timeless, theoretical question about the objective qualities of those words on that page. You are answering a time-bound, subjective but *factual* question: what happened in *you* when you read the words *this time*.

Pointing

Start by simply pointing to the words and phrases which most successfully penetrated your skull: perhaps they seemed loud or full of voice; or they seemed to have a lot of energy; or they somehow rang true; or they carried special conviction.

Any kind of getting through. If I have the piece of writing in my hand, I tend to put a line under such words and phrases (or longer passages) as I read. Later when telling my reactions, I can try to say which kind of getting through it was if I happen to remember. If I am listening to the piece read out loud, I simply wait till the end and see which words or phrases stick in my mind. I may jot them down as they come to me in the moments of silence after the readings.

Point also to any words or phrases which strike you as particularly weak or empty. Somehow they ring false, hollow, plastic. They bounced ineffectually off your skull. (I use a wavy line for these when I read with a pencil.)

Summarizing

Next summarize the writing:

a) First tell very quickly what you found to be the main points, main feelings, or centers of gravity. Just sort of say what comes to mind for fifteen seconds, for example, "Let's see, very sad; the death seemed to be the main event; um . . . but the joke she told was very prominent; lots of clothes."

b) Then summarize it into a single sentence.

c) Then choose *one word* from the writing which best summarizes it.

d) Then choose a word that isn't in the writing to summarize it.

Do this informally. Don't plan or think too much about it. The point is to show the writer what things he made stand out most in your head, what shape the thing takes in your consciousness. This isn't a test to see whether you got the words right. It's a test to see whether the words got you right. Be sure to use different language from the language of the writing. This insures that he is getting it filtered through your perception and experience—not just parroted. Also, try this test a week later: tell someone what you remember of his last week's piece.

Pointing and summarizing are not only the simplest ways to communicate your perception, but they are the most foolproof and the most useful. Always start with pointing and summarizing. If you want to play it safe and make sure your class is successful, or if you are terribly short of class time, or if your class is coming apart, try skipping all the following ways of giving feedback.

Telling

Simply tell the writer everything that happened to you as you tried to read his words carefully. It's usually easiest to tell it in the form of a story: first this happened, then this happened, then this happened, and so on. Here are two examples of telling (one concerning a story, the other a poem) from tape recordings of actual classes:

I felt confused about the man in the gray suit and the men gathered around you. I suppose they're cops, and the escorts. Because I had first thought the gray suit was a cop, but then I thought he was a dignified person who got arrested. I was uncertain about it. And then you talked about the men gathered around at one point—fairly early. I felt like they were cops, and I wanted you to contrast them to the fantasies. There was one point where you talked about—I think you were going down the stairs— and I felt like that whole part with the father of the bride and the gown was like the flash a person has, supposedly, when he's going to drown and his whole life flows before him. I thought it was like an initiation of a girl—or a woman, particularly—out of her whole parental, social, ball-gown past into this new thing. And

I was, I just, I was *surprised*. I didn't expect you to describe things that way. I was really happy. Then for some reason I felt like when you talked about the men who were gathered around—I felt like they were cops—and if I heard it again I might feel like I didn't need to have you say it, but at the time, as you said it, I wanted them to be blue suited or something contrasting. Perhaps that wouldn't be necessary for some other reader.

I had a very sort of happy feeling when you went to drinking songs. But it felt like the whole history of someone's life from being a young bride to becoming an old fishwife. I felt like it was a social comment in a way. One gets brought up and goes from the ideal fantasies to being fat and drinking companion in pubs. And I was just very happy at that change in age. It seemed like the whole thing was—if it were a movie it would be going around like this—but the history of a whole person in a way re-told in capsule form.

I didn't get into it till the middle section with the "one-two"s. I think I'd read down through the first two stanzas and didn't, um, not very much happened. In fact I think I felt it a little bit purple, a little bit corny, a little bit saying to myself "well he's having those nice thoughts, these nice words, but I can't go along, I'm not there." But I think even on first reading, when I got to the "one-two" business, I immediately picked up. Those words somehow made me pay attention. They became quite loud, there was a lot of—they really got me. I really listened to it as an interrogation. But for me it wasn't—as Mary said a minute ago—a standing back from emotions and being logical. It's not that it was so logical. It was like an interrogation, sort of. Like putting your feelings into this funny, numerical, pseudo-logical form. But it's quite hammering. I wrote down "the language is very real." Somehow it's moving. I don't take it as logic. I take it as some very insistent hammering thing.

And from then on I liked it. As I read down to the end I liked it fine. And when I got to the second page, I didn't even recognize that it was the same as the first page. I was starting to write down "I like this one much better," and when I went back to the first page to compare, I found the two were the same thing. In other words, after the "one-two"s, this thing really worked for me, and I got into it; those words got into my head; although "water brothers forever"—I remain slightly unclear about what to do with that line although it's sort of evocative.

And then the last three lines. Different handwriting, different mode. Again it was a kind of hammering: "Do you under*stand*." I didn't take it as something you were saying to a girl, I took it as something you were saying to yourself, or to the reader, or something. Sort of a kind of screaming. But screaming that works, not just screaming that's just sort of no good.

So then I went back. And when I saw that the first stanza was the same as the last stanza, I tried to figure out why I didn't like it so much the first time. And it was only then that I discovered that you had this great little device in the second stanza—repeating the first stanza with a new line interspersed every other line. I like that as an idea, but as far as the words go, they didn't work on me. I mean, once I perceived that pattern, I felt a kind of pleasure out of the pattern. I think patterns like that are fun. But I still couldn't like it as words. In particular the line "special cuz its hers": I didn't like it. I think part of it is that the abbreviation of 'because' into 'cuz' strikes me as corny and bothers me. It seems trivial but it's true. I don't know, I just didn't like it. "Seek and ye shall find" was maybe the one weak thing I didn't like in the "one-two" part. I ended up taking the whole thing very seriously as a poem.

The important thing in telling is not to get too far away from talking about the actual writing; people sometimes waste time talking only about themselves. But on the other hand, don't drift too far away from talking about yourself either, or else you are acting as though you are a perfectly objective, selfless critic.

To help you in telling, pretend that there is a whole set of instruments you have hooked up to yourself which record everything that occurs in you: not just pulse, blood pressure,

EEG, and so on, but also ones which tell every image, feeling, thought, and word that happens in you. Pretend you have hooked them all up and now you are just reading off the print-out from the machines.

Showing

When you read something, you have *some* perceptions and reactions which you are not fully aware of and thus cannot "tell." Perhaps they are very faint, perhaps you do not have satisfactory language for them, or perhaps for some other reason you remain unconscious of them. But though you cannot tell these perceptions and reactions, you can *show* them if you are willing to use some of the metaphorical exercises listed below. These may seem strange and difficult at first, but if you use them consistently you will learn to tap knowledge which you have but which is usually unavailable to you.

1. Talk about the writing as though you were describing *voices*: for example, shouting, whining, whispering, lecturing sternly, droning, speaking abstractedly, and so forth. Try to apply such words not only to the whole thing but to different parts.
2. Talk about the writing as though you were talking about *weather*: for example, foggy, sunny, gusty, drizzling, cold, clear, crisp, muggy, and so forth. Not just to the whole thing but to different parts.
3. Talk about the writing as though you were talking about *motion* or *locomotion*: for example, as marching, climbing, crawling, rolling along, tiptoeing, strolling, sprinting, and so forth.
4. *Clothing*: for example, jacket and tie, dungarees, dusty and sweaty shirt, miniskirt, hair all slicked down, etc.
5. *Terrain*: for example, hilly, desert, soft and grassy, forested, jungle, clearing in a forest, etc.

6. *Color:* what color is the whole? the parts?
7. *Shape.*
8. *Animals.*
9. *Vegetables.*
10. *Musical instruments.*
11. It is a *body:* what kind of body; which parts are feet, hands, heart, head, hair, etc.
12. Think of the piece of writing as having magically evolved out of a different piece of writing; and it will eventually evolve into some other piece of writing that again is different. Tell where it came from; where it is going.
13. Describe what you think was the writer's intention with this piece of writing. Then think of some crazy intention you think he might have had.
14. Assume that the writer wrote this *instead of* something very different that was really on his mind. Guess or fantasize what you think was really on his mind.
15. Assume that soon before he wrote this he did something very important or something very important happened to him—something that is not obvious from the writing. Say what you think it was.
16. Pretend this was written by someone you have never seen. Guess or fantasize what he or she is like.
17. The writing is a lump of workable clay. Tell what you would do with that clay.
18. Pretend to be someone else—someone who would have a very different response to the writing from what you had. Give this other person's perception and experience of the writing.
19. Quickly make the picture or doodle the writing inspires in you; pretend that the writing was received only by your arm with its pencil: now let them move.
20. Make the sound the writing inspires. Or imitate the sound of the writing. Different sounds for different parts.
21. Jabber it, that is, make the sound you would hear if someone was giving a somewhat exaggerated reading of it in the next room—in a language you had never heard (also compress it into 30 seconds or so).

22. Let your whole body make the movements inspired by the writing or different parts of it. Perhaps combine sounds and movements.
23. Do a ten-minute writing exercise on the writing and give it to the writer.
24. Meditate on the writing and try to tell him about what happened. Don't think about his writing. Try, even, to make your mind empty, but at the same time fully open to the writing. It's as though you don't chew and don't taste—just swallow it whole and noiselessly.

These showing procedures are not much use until you get over being afraid of them and unless you give two or three at a time. Therefore, I make it a rule that for your first four classes you make at least a couple of these oblique, metaphorical statements on each piece of writing. It may well feel strange and uncomfortable at first. Indeed, the reason I make this an explicit demand is that I have discovered that people in some trial teacherless classes were too timid to use them. In other classes where people did use them, almost everyone came to enjoy them and find them useful.

Don't struggle with them. Try to let the words just come. Say the thing that comes to mind even if it doesn't make any sense. And for the first few weeks, don't expect satisfactory results.

There's an easy way to think of the relation between telling and showing. Telling is like looking inside yourself to see what you can report. Showing is like installing a window in the top of your head and then taking a bow so the writer can see for himself. There's no need to try to remember what was happening as you read. Just bow. Showing conveys more information but in a more mixed and ambiguous form.

FURTHER ADVICE TO READERS

Make sure you've had a good chance to read the writing

Otherwise don't even start giving any reactions. If you read it silently in class, make sure you've had enough time to read it twice thoughtfully with a bit of time after each reading to let the words sink in and your impressions settle. *Don't let yourself be hurried.* If the writer reads it out loud, make sure he reads it twice and gives at least a whole minute of silence after each reading. And stop him whenever he reads too quickly or softly. A nervous writer may instinctively try to read it so no one can hear. Don't let him.

One reader at a time or all at once?

There is a lot to be said for each reader giving full movies of his mind—pointing, summarizing, telling, and showing—before any other reader starts in. This gives the writer not just a big mixed pile of reactions but rather a sense of each reader's experience as a whole. But on the other hand, sometimes it is easier for readers, especially in the first few weeks, if they can throw out reactions helter-skelter all together. Or you might do all the pointings, then all the summarizings, and so forth. There is no right way. Keep trying different ways to find what works best for your class.

As long as you are careful to tell your original reaction, it is also good to tell later reactions that may be different. Someone else's report may remind you of a perception you were having too but didn't realize it. Report it briefly even if it's the same as his. The writer needs to know whether a reaction is common or rare. Also someone may convey a perception or experience *different* from yours, but once you hear it you start to share it very strongly. It may blot out or supersede yours. This is also important to tell.

Never quarrel with someone else's reaction

If someone reports something that seems crazy, listen to him openly. Try to have his experience. Maybe what you see is truly there and he's blind. But maybe what he sees is there too. Even if it contradicts what you see. It is common for words to carry contradictory meanings and effects. What he sees may not be the main thing in the words, but because of his particular mood, temperament, or experience, it drowns out for him what you are seeing. Your position may blind you to what he sees. Your only chance of trying to sharpen your eyesight is to take seriously his seeming craziness and try to see what he sees. This may similarly encourage *him* to try to share what you see and thereby help make him a better reader too.

Give specific reactions to specific parts

Not just general reactions to the whole thing. You may have to make a special effort to do this. If you have trouble, try to think back and simply notice which particular passages you remember most. Point them out. Try to tell why you remember them, why they stick out, how you perceive and experience them. Do showing exercises on them. When you tell what happened—for example, "first this happened, then that happened"—try to point to specific places in the writing.

No kind of reaction is wrong

Insufficient, perhaps, but not wrong. There are certain kinds of reaction that don't *in themselves* help the writer much. But they are helpful if seen as part of the larger picture—part of the whole story of what it was like to be you and read his words carefully. So never struggle to *omit* any kind of response; struggle to include more. If it happened, tell it. Here are some kinds of reactions that some class members thought they were supposed to leave out:

1. Some classes got the impression from earlier drafts of this material that it was their business to talk about "how a person wrote something" but not "what he wrote." Not at all. The job is to find out what his words do to real people: *what* he is saying all mixed in with how he is saying it. If you want to quarrel with something the writer says, tell him (but don't go on to *have* the quarrel with him). There's no need to unscramble "style" and "content." Just tell what happened.

2. Odd reactions. Don't try to filter out the nutty parts and give only the "sensible" reactions. In fact it helps if you slightly exaggerate the craziness. It helps the writer break his habit of listening to feedback as though he were listening to his teacher. It makes him automatically realize he's not listening to even-handed judgments, conclusions, and advice—just one unique person's perceptions and experience. And it automatically helps you realize you are not trying to be God or a more-competent-than-everyone-else critic—just one person giving a slant that probably no one else could give. Your odd reactions will also help other readers just be themselves.

3. Advice. It's not valuable *as advice,* but it's valuable as part of the picture of how you experienced his words. Don't look for advice or try to think it up, but if the interaction between you and his words produces the desire to give advice, that's something the writer should know about. Sometimes a piece of

writing makes everyone want to give advice; whereas another piece of writing, though it's much less competent, doesn't inspire any advice at all. These are facts the writer needs to know.

Let your advice lead you to the perception or experience behind it. I often find that a desire to advise some change in something I'm reading is my only clue that I'm experiencing those words in a certain way. If I ask myself *why* I want to make the change, I can lead myself back to an interesting and useful perception of the words.

4. Evaluation. Like advice, evaluation in itself has no value. Don't try to figure out an evaluation, but on the other hand don't waste any energy trying to stop yourself. Give it and make it lead you to the perception and experience behind it. For example a teacher after three days of paper-grading sometimes reaches the point where his only response to a paper is to know what grade he wants to give it. This doesn't mean (necessarily) that there aren't rich perceptions tucked away behind that B minus. If such a teacher in such a state found himself in the teacherless writing class, he ought to start with the B minus and try to follow that string to find all the latent reactions behind it. What he should not do is to hide behind his evaluation and not tell his real experience.

Some people can't read without making judgments, other people seldom make any. The writer should get the feel of both kinds of reader. Even more interestingly, some pieces of writing somehow cry out for judgments—everyone's reaction is loud with them; whereas other pieces get themselves reacted to at great length with no evaluative talk at all.

One exception. I think it's worth banning negative judgments for the first three or four classes. When people get used to the class they can take the strongest kind of negative judgment in stride and learn from it without sweating it. But at the beginning people can be needlessly shaken. It's easy for four weeks simply to skip talking about what you didn't like.

5. Theories are less valuable than facts. But it's hard to keep the two apart. When you tell the writer what happened when you

read his words, you are telling him a fact. If you tell him why it happened—why you were bored here or confused there—you are telling him a theory about how language works or how you work. Your facts are much more trustworthy. It's *not* true that tons of adjectives always make writing boring; it's. *not* true that the passive voice is always weak; it's *not* true that abstractions are always vague; it's *not* true that examples always make things clearer. *In writing, anything can do anything.*

If *you* were bored by some adjectives, that's important; if *you* felt some particular passage as weak or vague, that's important; if *you* felt some example as helpful, that's important. Tell these things as happenings not theories. Your judgment about piles of adjectives in general, passive voice in general, abstractions in general, examples in general is not worth much. No one's is.

The trouble is that it is hard to keep theories apart from facts. Not only do some of your best facts only come when you uncork your dubious theories; *all* your facts are probably slightly polluted by your theories. If you think flowery writing is weak in general, you probably fool yourself into experiencing all flowery writing as weaker than you otherwise would. So you might as well let your theories show—so the writer can see how to distrust you. Here again, the moral is the same; your theories are not valuable in themselves, but they help give the writer a better sense of what it was like to be you as you read his words.

6. Seemingly irrelevant reactions. For example: "As I read it, all I could think about was what I'm going to do tomorrow" (or what I did yesterday, or how hot it is in here, or the fact that I'm bored by that subject). You might say these are not perceptions of the words at all but rather failures to perceive them. Yet it is crucial to give this sort of reaction. The main thing is that these responses occurred when you read the words and your job is to tell what happened. Perhaps it's your "fault" that you didn't perceive them more, that you daydreamed. Perhaps you should try harder. But there's no way of figuring out whose fault it is. The main fact is that he put words on paper

that were supposed to get into your head and they did not. Different readers often daydream at the same points in the writing—a clue that something funny is probably going on there.

There may be many such irrelevant reactions at the beginning of this kind of class. People are not used to giving reactions; they are self-conscious about it; they feel awkward trying to listen to something read out loud. Nevertheless, if it happened, tell it. This will free you to notice other perceptions that were hidden behind the irrelevant one.

But supposedly irrelevant reactions are not just good for their side-effects. In the majority of cases they are good feedback in themselves. *The basic fact about most verbal utterance is that it doesn't get through.* The main story of words interacting with people is the story of ideas and experiences falling useless on the ground or only faintly heard through the fog; people pretending they heard something when really they only saw someone's mouth moving and guessed what he was saying from the circumstances and the expression on his face. I've discovered that many classes try to ignore this primal fact. Readers try to tell the writer what they perceive or experience, but they are fishing and fumbling and making things up. They don't dare tell the most valuable reaction there is: "I didn't really hear a thing you said." It's no fun to get that reaction if you are the writer. But in the end it's a relief to have out on the table what you suspected was true all along.

> *Though no reactions are wrong,*
> *you still have to try to read well*

The class is not an invitation to be merely lazy, sloppy, passive—a bad reader. In one of the teacherless classes I listened to on tape, one man said of a woman's essay, "I stopped reading after the first paragraph. I said the hell with it. It seemed to me like one of those essays in the *Sunday Times Magazine.* I figure if I want to read one of those things, I'll go read it in the *Sunday Times Magazine*." Now that's a good statement of *what happened* when he read the first paragraph. It's a useful thing to say (though not much fun to hear). He doesn't explain why he is so mad at the piece, but that's all right: it's not his job to psychoanalyze himself or to theorize about how words work. He localized his reaction to the first paragraph. That's good.

The trouble is he didn't read the rest. That's no fair. He should have kept reading. Perhaps his reactions would have changed. But even if they didn't, the perceptions of a hostile reader are useful.

When I took literature courses in college I remember that my main experience in reading was the feeling that I ought to have the right reactions. But I could never figure out what they were. I could scarcely think about what I was reading because I was always worrying about having the wrong reactions. This was no way to be a good reader. I had eventually to learn to be, *in a sense*, more passive and irresponsible—to relax and not worry and let the words do what they want to do. But that doesn't mean I can just sit back and be passive and wait for the words to pick me up and carry me. To be a good reader I must supply great effort, attention, and energy.

Sometimes you may not want to

If you sometimes find you simply don't want to give your reactions, and you don't know why but you just start to clam up and have nothing to say, respect these feelings. They are appropriate. To give movies of your mind is an act of extreme generosity, self-abnegation. You are making yourself a meter, a guinea pig, a laboratory. You're letting the writer use you as a tool for his own ends. For example, perhaps you think his piece is much too long and complicated. If, along with this opinion, you give him movies of your mind and tell him all the perceptions and feelings that are involved (that is, where did it start? were you actually perplexed or annoyed or just disapproving? and so on) you are giving him the opportunity to decide that length and complexity are not really the problem at all. By seeing your reactions more fully, he may even decide that he doesn't need to heed them. *And he may be right.* Yet he can't make this decision well unless you give him all your reactions and not just your conclusions. If you had told him *only* your judgment, you would have been invulnerable and he would have had to like it or lump it.

So it's no joke, this kind of feedback. You wouldn't be human if there weren't some occasions when you didn't feel like it. You might as well admit it. Even act on those feelings and don't tell your reactions. Say you are tired of it at the moment, you pass. This is much better than fooling yourself and going on to give responses that are really a smokescreen.

You are always right and always wrong

You do your job as reader best in the light of this paradox.

You are always right in that no one is ever in a position to tell you what you perceive and experience. You must have a kind of faith or trust: not that your perception is always accurate, but that the greatest accuracy comes from using it more and listening to it better; and that the most valuable thing you can do for the writer is tell him what you really see and how you really react.

But you are always wrong in that you never see accurately enough, experience fully enough. There are always things in the words you cannot get. You must always put more energy into trying to have other people's perceptions and experi-ences—trying to make yourself more agile, more flexible, more refined. Don't stubbornly stay locked into your own impres-sions just because they are yours.

In short, you must be simultaneously sure of yourself and humble. Easier said than done. But it's worth the practice this class provides since it's just what's needed in countless other situations.

ADVICE TO THE WRITER ON LISTENING

Be quiet and listen

For many weeks you may have to bite your tongue. If you talk you'll keep readers from telling you important reactions. Don't give long introductions. In fact, you may learn more if the readers are a little uncertain what the writing is, what it is meant for, who it is aimed at. If they cannot comfortably pigeon-hole it, they may take less for granted and notice more.

You have to keep from making apologies or exlanations, for example, "I just wrote this last night, I didn't have much time and didn't revise it at all"; or "I'm really not satisfied with this"; or "I finally got this the way I want it, but I had to do four drafts." Above all, never say what you want your writing to do, how you want your readers to respond. You'll destroy any chance of getting trustworthy evidence of whether you did it. After you get your audience to tell you how they themselves perceived it, *then* you can ask them how they think some different audience might respond.

As they are telling you their experience, you have to guard against being tricked into responding; that is, "What do you mean you were confused about the point of this paragraph? I

wrote right in the first sentence that . . ." After the reactions
are in, you can explain what you intended or what you think
you've put in it. People will ask you questions: "Why did you
do such and such?" "What did you mean here?" Don't answer
till after you get their reactions. Get them to tell you what
perception, feeling, or uncertainty made them ask. Such questions are often a clue to a reaction that the reader is not otherwise conscious of.

Don't try to understand what people tell you

It will be a mess. Contradictory, incomplete, seemingly non-
sensical. Just listen and take it all in. If you try to learn by
understanding, you will cut yourself out of half the learning.
Your organism as a whole is capable of benefitting from much
more than you can understand.

But do try to understand HOW they tell it to you

You can't ask for all the useful information on a silver platter.
Notice *how* people tell you about their experience of your
words. Sometimes they aren't in a position to say, "Your
words made me annoyed at you," but if you only listen you'll
see that your words *did* annoy them. Or put them in a good
mood. Or made them feel condescending. Or made them feel
like not really taking your words seriously. Take it in.

Don't reject what readers tell you

Listen to what they say *as though it were all true*. The way an
owl eats a mouse. He takes it all in. He doesn't try to sort out
the good parts from the bad. He trusts his organism to make

use of what's good and get rid of what isn't. There are various ways in which a reader can be wrong in what he tells you; but still it pays you to accept it all:

1. If he gives you mere evaluations, advice about changes to make, or theories about writing, these are of no value to you in themselves. But don't try to stop him. It will just hang him up and prevent him from going on to tell you more about how he perceived and experienced your words. And besides, if you listen sensitively, you can feel *behind* his evaluation, advice, and theory what the rest of his reactions were like and what it was like to be him reading your words.

2. A reader *can* be mistaken about his own reactions. For example, someone can think he scorns a piece of writing or is bored by it or doesn't understand it when really he is threatened by it but won't let himself feel threatened. You can't eliminate this kind of error, only minimize it. The way to minimize it is to be as open and accepting a listener as possible in order to help the person hear and accept his real reactions.

3. If a reader fails to see or experience something that you are almost certain is in there, in this respect he is wrong. He is blind. He couldn't see something right there in front of his face. But don't make the mistake of concluding that he's therefore wrong about what he says he *does* see. Words usually contain many effects and even contrary meanings. The usefulness of the class is in bringing to light the whole range of possible effects and meanings in this set of words. There may be something very faintly in the words which this reader's situation makes him experience as dominant, but which none of the other readers can see. Of course it may *not* be there. But your only chance of benefiting is to take it in without trying to distinguish the wrong parts.

   In fact you should practice a kind of mystical discipline: assume the perceptions or experiences that seem most crazy are really most useful. Those perceptions you need most—that is, those you are least capable of having yourself because of your particular point of view—will naturally seem most crazy to you.

Don't stop them from giving you reactions

If you are not learning much about how they really reacted it is probably your fault. Not theirs. If you are too afraid of hearing how they really experience your words, that fear will come across and they will find some way of not telling you. Also if you don't really listen or take them seriously, that will get across and they will withhold reactions. If you oversimplify and pigeon-hole everybody—saying to yourself, "this is the grammar nut, this is the sentimental one, this is the overly logical one"—this too is a way of not really litsening to them: defending yourself against really having their experience. They will feel it and hold back.

But don't be tyrannized by what they say

You've got to listen openly and take it in, but not be paralyzed or made helpless by it. Otherwise you will *scare* them into holding back. There's a kind of tacit agreement in any good feedback situation: they agree to transmit to you everything that happened *only if* they can see you won't be bamboozled by it.

Suppose they all agree that something you wrote is profoundly lousy. Be clear what that means. It means it didn't work for them. They couldn't get to it or it couldn't get to them. It *doesn't* necessarily mean it's lousy. It might be good. Some of the greatest pieces of writing are hated by most people. Don't look to your readers to find out whether your words are any good. Look to them to find out about what your words make happen in real consciousnesses. The better you get at feeling how your words affect consciousnesses, the better you will be at deciding *for yourself* whether your words are any good.

Suppose some readers think your writing is too sentimental (or too unclear, too intellectual, too ordinary, too whatever). What does this mean? It probably means they were bothered by the sentimentality. But you can bet they sometimes love things that are twice as sentimental (or unclear, etc.) The complaint might disappear entirely if you made some *other* change—perhaps something quite small that has nothing to do with sentimentality. That is why it is no use trying to figure it all out. Just take it all in. Assume that when you write something else—or rewrite this piece—your *own* choices about how to write it will organically benefit from hearing what they are now saying.

Remember who has what job. It's their job to give you their experience. It's your job to decide what to do next. If you start putting decision-making power into their hands, you push yourself out of the picture.

It's not their job to decide what's in your head or even on the page—merely what got into their heads. It's not their job to be fair. It's not their job to cushion you from harsh or incorrect perceptions. If they try to do that, they cannot do their main job of giving you their experience. It's not their job to play teacher or God and try to tell you what the words *might* do if this or that were different. If they get into the business of trying to tell you what other words *might* do, they'll lose their capacity to tell you what these words *did* do. (This is how teachers get into trouble.)

Ask for what you want, but don't play teacher with them

If there's some particular kind of feedback you find helpful, perhaps certain kinds of oblique, metaphorical statements from the "showing" list, ask them. Or ask them, if you wish, for their experience of some particular passage or aspect of your writing. Ask in such a way that they can decline.

But you will defeat yourself if you try to play teacher: asking them leading questions, helping them along, "conducting" them. If someone hasn't managed to give you movies of his mind, tell him. But don't try to tell him how to fix the situation. That's his job. He's the one who can find the best solution even though it might take a number of weeks.

You are always right and always wrong

You, as writer, as well as reader, benefit most if you listen in the spirit of this paradox.

You are always right in that your decision about the writing is always final. They give you their experience, you decide what to do about it. You are in charge. You are the only one making decisions.

But you are always wrong in that you can never quarrel with their experience—never quarrel even with their report of their experience. And you must assume that you are never good enough at sharing their perception—shedding your blinders, getting into their shoes.

Like the reader, you must be simultaneously sure of yourself and humble.

THE CLASS PROCESS

I've been developing this kind of class over a long period; trying things out in my own classes; and listening to tapes of experimental teacherless classes which used earlier versions of this material. Some classes went well, some adequately, and some pooped out.

Take what follows not as a satisfactory or sufficient map of the path ahead but rather as my attempt to tell you everything I know. You will still feel lost some of the time. It is how I often continue to feel when I participate in this kind of class.

Supplying the ingredients

If you do the following things, you will prevent what I see as the most frequent problems:

Get a commitment from at least seven people for a ten-week stretch

Make sure everyone writes something every week

Make sure everything read out loud is read twice and given a minute's silence after each reading

Give pointing and summarizing responses to every piece of writing

Make sure everyone, for his first four classes, uses two showing exercises for transmitting his reactions

Do three ten-minute writing exercises each week

Use the last five minutes of each class for reactions to the class itself

Motivation

The main thing this class demands is that you really want to work on your writing. In a regular class you can play this kind of game with the teacher: "Please, teacher, I want to make my writing better. But I don't want to work. Please make me *want* to work. Or if you can't do that, at least *make* me work and let me resent you for it." People who are playing games with themselves may come to exploratory meetings but they won't commit themselves for ten weeks if you make the commitment clear. Soon you have a group of people who really mean business. It's a pleasure.

Down to business

Business is a useful concept here. This class reminds some people of an encounter group because it makes such central use of the reactions of the members. But an encounter group has no business or agenda: whatever comes up is business; there is no such thing as wasting time. That's not true in the teacherless writing class. Here there is definite business. Each piece of writing must get reactions. The job to be done gives a kind of structure and solidity.

Patience

Though you have to want results and mean business, you can't be in a hurry. Improving your writing is necessarily gradual and erratic. The teacherless class isn't necessarily slower than a regular class but it usually *seems* slower. A teacher can give you something to do and someone to trust while waiting for the slow underground learning to take place. For example, he might tell you to stop using so many adjectives and long sentences, to start using more concrete details, and to give more unity to your paragraphs. Here's something to think about, something to try to do. In a sense it is good advice. You may even make progress toward these goals. By the fifth week you might be able to say to yourself, "Yes,

I guess my writing isn't perfect yet, but at least I've gotten rid of some of the adjectives and long sentences, put in some concrete details and paragraph unity." This makes *everybody* feel much better. The trouble is your writing may actually be no better. In a sense worse. True, it's closer to someone's *model* of good writing, but very likely it is no better at actually putting things inside real readers. Besides, these "improvements" probably stop when the course is over.[3] The real process by which you generate words is probably unchanged. Writing is probably harder, more painful and more confusing because you're now trying to do certain new things yet your word-production process is unchanged. It's no accident that many people stop writing when they start being taught how to write better.

It takes a long time for the organism to learn new ways of generating words—better ways to make words actually get through to other people. You must be ready for long dry spells, setbacks, and spurts forward when you least expect them. (See the next chapter for a fuller treatment of the learning process.) But remember what you often get from a teacher. He spurs and encourages you: "Don't give up; I know you are discouraged, but keep it up, things are going fine." He is someone to trust. And in some learning situations he can force you to keep going. Learn here to get this support and encouragement—coercion if needs be—from yourself and from the others. It's harder, but when you do it, there is great excitement because you have tapped a new energy source that is extremely powerful and effective.

And while you are working at it, learn to have fun. Enjoy

3. This is one of the findings in *Themes, Theories, and Therapy,* the Report of the Dartmouth Study of Student Writing, Albert Kitzhaber, McGraw Hill, 1963.

getting to know the others well. Trying to see through their eyes is a good way. Enjoy, almost as a game, the feedback process. Think of the class as a group of amateur musicians who get together once a week to play for each other's enjoyment.

A different style of interaction

This class asks you to function with others in a way you are probably not used to. Unless you can change a few crucial gears, the class will fold. I've seen it happen in a number of experimental teacherless classes I've monitored. I can specify better now what those gears are that you need to change.

In a sense it is simply a matter of not arguing. You can argue someone out of an incorrect intellectual position (sometimes). But you can't argue someone out of an incorrect perception or experience. He only discards one when he already has another to replace it with. And the new one must be one *he* is already having and believing, not one being rammed down his throat by someone else. In short, if you want to improve someone's perception or experience, you can't do it by arguing. The best you can do is to persuade him to share yours. The only way to do this, almost invariably, is to go over and share his.

But there's something more central to focus on than arguing. It is the cause of arguing: the impulse to *settle* things, *decide* things. When we are in any class or meeting we tend to feel that the goal is to achieve agreement. We habitually feel frustrated if we have a discussion with great difference of opinion but no final agreement.

The teacherless class asks you to break out of this habit. It brings out the *maximum* differences but it asks you not to

fight things out or try to settle on the truth. Only by inhibiting the compulsive urge to settle things can you bring out
the maximum differences. The striking thing about most
classes, meetings, and discussions—especially in comparison to
a functioning teacherless class—is that there is usually such a
poverty of difference, a poverty of disagreement. Who wants
to ruffle things up when it is all for the purpose of having
things smoothed down again in exactly fifty minutes? Who
wants to play thesis or antithesis to someone's planned syn-
thesis? And even when there is a heated fight, it is usually a
fight between two polarized, narrow possibilities. A whole
host of interesting points of view have never been raised because there is such an atmosphere of needing to settle things.
It's only by tolerating *a lot* of ambiguity for a long time, by
living with *a lot* of contradiction, and inhibiting the need to
settle things too soon that you can get your hands on a decent
array of data.

So keep two danger signals in mind: the two directions a
class is apt to slide in when too many people can't handle
their urge always to settle things.

1. *People persist in arguing.* They get mad and waste a lot
   of time trying to decide what is true. Or else they force
   themselves to stop overt arguments, but you can feel them
   still doing it underground. In their heads they're saying,
   "How can that idiot be so wrong, so blind? What's the
   matter with him? How come he doesn't admit he's wrong
   and agree with what I said? He's so *stupid!*" Such underground fuming is exhausting and wastes all available energy and the class breaks down.
2. *Or else people* don't *argue.* But stopping argument feels to
   them like a huge giving-in, capitulation. The wind has

been taken out of their sails. It feels to them like a merely random, utterly relaxed, gutless activity: "Well, if we're not going to argue things out, if anyone can get away with saying anything he wants, if no one is going to stop people from shooting off their mouths with utter nonsense, then I'll just say what I want, the rest can say what they want. Who the hell cares." Because normal paths for energy are closed off, they withdraw all energy. The class is merely slack, relaxed, boring, unfocussed. It dies.

So the main thing I have finally been able to center on is the peculiar quality of energy and attention this class asks for. It's a great effort. But instead of being directed towards arguing and settling—toward closure—energy must be expended in the opposite direction of keeping oneself open, listening, trying to have other people's experiences—in a sense trying to *agree* with everyone at once. What it feels like, when it goes well, is a sense of attention, of tautness, of great energy invested into one's perceiving and experiencing muscles—all the while keeping the mind from making its instinctive clench.

Bravery

What I hear loudest in the tape of a good teacherless class is bravery. Willingness to risk. The teacherless class makes people nervous. They are on their own. There is no one there who has been there before to tell them when they are doing things right, to reassure them. It's almost as though I can hear someone saying to himself, "Well, it's no use waiting for someone else to do it for us. There's no one special to lead the way. I guess someone has to start. I'll give it a try." And he takes the risk of really sharing his perception and experience.

It is a kind of ice-breaking operation that makes it possible for the others to follow. They discover that nothing terrible happens to the first person. When a class can't get itself going, what I feel is everyone hanging back, waiting for someone else.

This ice-breaking is not once-and-for-all. People don't plunge immediately into utter honesty. A successful class seems characterized by a series of small breakthroughs over a long time. By many increments, they work up to sharing fuller and fuller reactions to the words.

If you want to insure that a class gets going, try to find brave people to be in it: people who are willing to say what they see and feel, and not worry so much about how others will view it. Young children are useful members of a class.

Responsibility

In most regular classes you feel a responsibility toward the teacher, not toward the other members of the class. When you are wavering between going or not going, think how often the inner debate is in terms of "what will the teacher say or think if I don't come." All too often it is *only* the thought of the teacher that gets us to come to class.

With this background, it is hard to learn responsibility to peers. This is why I emphasize the commitment for ten weeks. It takes that long for most people to transfer their responsibility from a teacher to themselves and their peers—to feel and communicate that their learning depends on each other.

When a class works, you can feel people sticking up for themselves; making genuine demands and expectations of others that their time not be wasted, that they learn something. When a class fails, you can feel people failing to take responsibility for themselves. Saying, in effect, "What can I do; I'm helpless; my only choice is to quit."

Although you cannot entirely change the world or trans-form people at a stroke, this class makes it perfectly obvious that you *can* change instantaneously the way eight or ten people act toward you for a couple of hours a week. If a person has a tendency to talk too much or be bossy, you cannot re-verse his personality. But in this class you can stop him from cheating you with his talking and bossiness for a couple of hours a week. You have only to want it and stick up for your-self by insisting on it politely but firmly. The threatening thing about this class is that it faces people with the fact that they are not so helpless as they prefer to think. The idea that classes must always have teachers reinforces helplessness.

How to destroy the class secretly

Here's the most common way this sort of class breaks down. Everyone is a bit nervous and even frightened because it's such a strange and unsettling enterprise. It's almost inevi-table. In this situation, what's most soothing is to find some-one who likes to talk: someone who likes to ramble on with personal anecdotes, someone who likes to make speeches, or someone who is nervous when there's a silence and just drones on to fill it up. From here it's easy. You just let him go. En-courage him, but not openly. Just let opportunities occur. And most of all, refrain from stopping him from boring you. Pretend you are extremely polite.

Everyone starts saying to himself, "Boy, what a drag this class is! That person just talks and talks. He's ruining it. I can't stand it much longer." This feeling gets in the air and then a couple of people sort of drop out. That is, they don't quite drop out so that you could ask them about it; it's just that important things somehow start coming up to conflict with class meetings. Then everyone can start saying, "Boy this class is discouraging! It feels like it's falling apart. Everyone is down. I'm really discouraged. By the way, I just remembered, I've got an important meeting I've got to go to when the class next meets."

Finally the class breaks up. Maybe you've already dropped out or maybe you're there at the end supposedly feeling bad and supposedly wondering why other people can't stick with something. And you can blame it all conveniently on the poor sucker you got to cooperate with you by being a bore when you invited him to. You couldn't stand letting others enjoy what was too scary for you so you helped destroy it—but secretly. Everyone blames him. He even blames himself. No one blames you.

The moral of the process is that you must take responsibility for what happens in class: if you don't really try to stop it, you must want it to happen.

Diversity

A functioning class exploits the differences *between* individuals to pry open more diversity *within* individuals. When everyone tries to have everyone else's perception and experience, richness is continually plowed back into the group. There is a constantly growing potential for diversity of experience.

But it is not foolproof. I'm sad to say I've seen one teacherless class drift in the opposite direction: toward a sense of conformity, group ideology. Watch out for any drift toward unspoken ideas that certain kinds of feeling or writing are more acceptable than others: for example, that simplicity is good and complexity is bad; that strong feelings are good and lack of strong feelings is bad; or that seriousness is good, frivolity is bad. It's simply wrong. It's a result of insecurity or fear. The whole usefulness of a group is to reinforce the only trustworthy theory about writing: anything is possible. It's what e. e. cummings meant by the old vaudeville line, "Would you hit a lady with a baby?" "If I had to, I'd hit her with a baseball bat!" In writing, anything can work and anything is right if you make it work.

5

Thoughts on the Teacherless Writing Class

THE main idea behind the teacherless writing class is that you can't trust theory, you can only trust facts. The only trouble is that you can't get away from theory. Facts are always dirty with some theory: no one can "see a fact" or "say what really happened" without using an implicit model or theory. On top of everything else, I love theories and models so much that I wouldn't leave them out if I could.

As I tried to write about the teacherless writing class, I was constantly derailed by digressions into theory-making and model-building. I finally realized I should collect it all here.

HOW I CAME TO THIS APPROACH

The main thing has been my experience as a teacher trying to comment on student papers. During my first years as a teacher, my head would swim and I'd become completely baffled as I tried to think of useful things to say about student papers. But after a number of years this changed. Slowly I developed a more or less firm and communicable idea of what I was looking for: clear, not-too-wordy sentences; paragraphs

each organized around a clear, discrete point; a shaped or logical structure to the whole thing; and adequacy of argument
and documentation. These standards could probably be
called the main academic line in rhetorical taste: clean writing—writing that tries to call more attention to its message
than to itself.

At last I knew what I was doing when I graded and com-
mented on papers. No longer the nightmare of groping in the
dark. I knew what a good paper was. I felt justified in using
these standards because they weren't too narrow or idiosyncratic. I felt I could specify where a paper fell down and what
changes the writer should make. As long as my unspoken
premises held together it seemed to me I was a competent and
useful commenter.

But my premises didn't hold together. After some years it
began to happen that I would find myself in the middle of
writing a comment and begin to wonder whether it could
really be trusted, whether it was really useful. Perhaps I was
telling someone about his flowery and wordy diction. His diction was indeed wordy and could be called flowery. But I began to wonder if this was *why* I was complaining about it. I
sometimes found myself suspecting it was something else I
couldn't put my finger on that bothered me but floweriness
was more available. If I were in a different mood or the paper
were in a different place in the stack, perhaps I wouldn't have
made the comment I did.

Or sometimes the floweriness did seem to be the culprit
but in a peculiar way: he was having such fun writing it and
any reader who was in the right frame of mind could also have
fun reading it. But I, in my writing, *can't* have fun with this
kind of diction, and in my reading I don't seem to be able to
have fun with it; and so it makes me mad.

Or perhaps I was pointing out the flaws in someone's organization or argument. But something made me realize I was really *looking* for something the matter. I could probably find other papers with similar structure I didn't complain of. I could even imagine being very sympathetic and persuaded by just such an argument—could find just such an organization clear—if other circumstances had been different. These things *could* be called flaws, yet the more I thought about it, the more it seemed that these professional, objective matters of diction, paragraphing, organization, and argument *weren't what determined how I responded to the paper.*

But if I tried to say *how* and *why* I actually did respond, I was immediately out of bounds: it was all mixed up with my mood and my personal quirks or taste and my temperament. It wouldn't seem fair either. I would clearly like some papers that seemed to me worse than others, and hate some that seemed really quite good.

My frustration grew and I finally said what the hell. If there is something fishy in my attempt to be fair and objective, how about trying to be as subjective as I can. So then I became intrigued with trying to be good at being subjective: actually trying to give a full and accurate report of what went on in me as a result of reading the words on the paper: no matter how little I understood why I was having these thoughts and feelings and even if they seemed nutty.

I found this was no easier than trying to be objective. All my habits worked against me. Sometimes I didn't know what my reactions were. And often I felt odd and vulnerable trying to tell reactions when I didn't understand why I was having them. No doubt I often missed the real truth about my reactions. But the new struggle seemed better. I felt it made the whole transaction between writer and reader much

more genuine. I felt it helped the student's writing a bit
more. It was much more fun. And it seemed to increase my
powers of perception: simply to start writing a comment of
this sort often led me to notice something about the paper
that was very interesting—and helpful to the student—but
something I never would have noticed if I had stuck with
trying to be fair, professional, and objective.

In other words, when my teaching began, I had an experience of the student's paper, but I had no idea what to tell the
student. But then I gradually moved farther away from my
experience of the paper: instead of noticing my reactions, I
noticed where the writing fit my model of good writing and
praised those parts, and noticed where it departed from my
model of good writing and criticized those parts, and told the
student how to make improvements. I could afford to ignore
my experience and reactions because at last I had a workable
model. And it was a great relief—not just because I finally felt
I had something useful to say, but because it's too exhausting
to experience and react to a stack of 20, 40, or 60 papers. To
bring to bear the whole organism and all its reactors is too
much. To bring a good model to bear is much easier, much
more sanity-conserving. When I got good at it, I found I
could often short-circuit the experiencing process altogether:
simply notice diction, paragraphing, organization, and argument, and not experience the paper at all. And still apply the
model well.

I would also use the model with respect to "content"—not
just form or style. When there are a lot of papers, it's hard
actually to experience each person's whole argument. It's
easier simply to hold it up against one's own model of what
the argument should be. That's why so much essay grading
and commenting is a process whereby the teacher "checks off"

the "points" a student makes against a kind of inner master list. In short, there is a terrific pressure for the English teacher to minimize his experience of a set of words and maximize his construction of a model (perhaps implicit) in order to check off a piece of writing against it. And so, bit by bit, one *has* less and less experience of a set of words that one could transmit to a student.

When I finally embarked on trying to transmit my experience of his words, it didn't take me long to realize that it would be better if the student could get the experience of more than one reader. He would get a wider range of reactions to offset the onesidedness of a single reaction. And so I began to try to get the whole class to give reactions in this way.

Another experience confirmed this approach for me. During this period I participated in a couple of encounter groups and joined a therapy group conducted by a psychoanalyst. In these settings I often learned other people's reactions to something I said and suddenly realized that I had just learned more about that piece of speech than I usually was able to learn about words I had written on paper. This feedback consisted of people telling what the words had made happen in them.

HUH?

I've often had a kind of surreal, underwater vision of social reality. It usually seemed as though this was a purely private and aberrant experience. But now the teacherless class reinforces it.

Everyone walks around mostly out of communication with

everyone else. Someone has turned off the sound, cut the wires. It's all fog and silence. If we really said what we were feeling in many situations, it would be, "Did you say something? I thought maybe I saw your mouth moving, but I wasn't sure. I guess you did look sort of worked up."

We don't admit this Faulknerian vision. We pretend we heard and understood words when we only saw the other person's mouth move. In fact I think that the fear of honest feedback is not so much a fear that the other person will think us wrong, childish, evil, or stupid. Those are easy to take in comparison with our worst fear: that our words were not heard at all; or that they were perceived as merely random, meaningless babble; that the only honest feedback an audience could give would be to stare at us uncomprehendingly, mouth slightly open, and say, "Huh?"

It's usually only adolescents and people in emotional crises who go around saying, "No one understands me! No one understands what I am trying to say!" For it is they who most need to send complex messages about the way they feel and the way they perceive the world, and to have these messages understood. Most of the rest of us discover that only simple, trivial messages get through and so we give up sending complicated ones. Pass the salt. What's playing at the movies? Where are you going tomorrow? We no longer try to describe important things like what life is like and how we live and what we need. That's why it is so magical when you have a friend who actually understands much of what you are trying to say. It makes you want to say things you never thought you had in you.

I see all this in the classes now. At first people try to be polite and nice. They try to think they hear and understand messages. But before long a couple of brave souls finally say it. "Huh?" Here's this long piece of language: probably carefully and painfully written. They see mouths moving and hear noises, but really they can't understand a thing.

This is frustrating for the writer, but it is also a relief. At last what he suspected all along is out on the table. Finally, there is no longer this pretence that communication is going on. Finally one can get down to business and notice the stray phrase or passage that actually *does* get through. There is no hope of separating real communication from static when people pretend that the whole thing is communication.

When noncommunication is more out in the open, good communication can begin. People eventually start to hear each other very well. This explains something about these classes that had perplexed and even perturbed me. When I set up a writing class or invited people to join one, I often put a big emphasis on pragmatic writing—committee reports, letters, writings for a job, writing essays for some other class: trying to make words do a real-live job where you can tell in a concrete way whether they have done the job you wanted. I'm not a "creative writing" person and I've always felt insecure about it. But I've found that many people who start a course with a desire to work on pragmatic kinds of writing, as I had encouraged them to do, begin after a while to ignore these goals and move toward more personal, imaginative, or creative writing. Now I think I know why. When people not only begin to improve their writing ability but also find themselves in a group where their words are heard and understood better than they usually are, they discover messages they want to send which they had forgotten were on their minds. They want to say things that are complex and difficult to express which they had previously learned to ignore because it had always been impossible to get them heard.

WHY THE TEACHERLESS CLASS
HELPS MAKE WRITING EASIER

Most people can learn to write much more easily. This does not solve all their problems. Perhaps they still write badly. But now they write. Now they get pleasure from writing. They write more and this too helps their writing. And they can direct more energy into trying to write well instead of needing it all—and then some—simply to get words down.

There are two conditions that help you produce words easily. These two conditions are usually absent when you write but the teacherless class helps to produce them.

The first condition is to know how people are reacting to your words. Usually you know this when you are having a conversation with someone, and so you don't find it hard to speak meaningfully and fluently. Before you go on to the second thing you have to say, you get a feel for how your listener reacted to the first thing. You can tell not only from what he says but from how he says it—little physical movements and postures—whether he is understanding you, whether he agrees with you at all, or whether he is beginning to think you are crazy.

Think of peculiar speaking situations in which you don't know how a listener is reacting to your words. It is much harder to produce meaningful speech. There is a bit of this problem when you are talking to an absolute stranger. He is hard to "read." He might have very different responses from those you are used to. When you get *no* clues, speaking is especially difficult. Perhaps the person is paralyzed, or he is from such a foreign culture that you can't read him at all, or he is a social scientist conducting an experiment in withholding feedback, or perhaps he is just a psychiatrist. Sometimes you actually talk *more* during the first moments of such a situation: the silence is so embarrassing that you babble a bit. But usually words soon dry up.

In writing, however, this is the normal condition. No wonder it is agony. As you are writing you get no clues as to how readers will react. You have to write the whole thing out, keep going till the end, even though you have no idea whether the reader is lost or thinks you are crazy at the end of the first paragraph. Not only that, you don't even know *who* will read it. Once your words are on paper, they can be easily transported before the eyes of anyone—no matter how you feel about him, no matter how little he knows or understands you. (Notice how often people use metaphors of nakedness to describe what it feels like when they write.) In writing, there is only one way to be sure who will read it: rip it up and throw it in the wastebasket. No wonder that's what usually happens.

The teacherless class comes as close as possible to taking you out of the dark about how your words are experienced, and thus making it easier to produce meaningful words on paper.

There's another condition that makes it easy to produce language: *not worrying* how the audience experiences your words.

There are times when you simply have to speak out. The chips are down. Damn the torpedoes. It's the only way to maintain your very integrity or self-respect. In such situations, once you have started, you are usually surprised how fluent (and powerful) your words are.

Most people, no matter how hard it is ordinarily for them to write, have had one or two experiences of this sort when writing came easily. Perhaps it was an important personal

letter in which you finally had to say how you felt no matter
what the consequences. Perhaps it was a written test where
desperation and not-caring added up right, so you could say,
"Well, what the hell." Perhaps it was a paper that was so late
you finally had to stop worrying about how it would be perceived. This is why so many people can only write something
when it is overdue. Sometimes only desperation is powerful
enough to make you stop worrying about how your words will
be received.

The teacherless class will also help you reach this blessed
state of not worrying, if you stick with it for a while. At first
the class makes you depend on all this feedback you are getting: you wonder how you wrote anything before without it.
But after a while you don't care about it so much. After a
while you get enough reactions from enough people that finally you begin to develop a trustworthy sense of the effects
of your words. You have learned the feel of real readers. For
another thing, the class helps you worry less about whether
people *like* what you wrote. You notice that in most cases it
is impossible to please everyone. People's reactions are too
different. There's no piece of writing in the world that would
please everyone in the class. You eventually learn that it's not
even very useful to learn someone's judgment of your words
compared to learning his perceptions and experiences of
them. So instead of letting the standards of the readers call
the shots for you, gradually you come to make your own decisions as to what is good and bad, and use the responses of
others to help you fulfill *your own* goals, not their goals. You
are interested in their responses and you learn from them, but
you no longer worry about them. This nonworrying frees
your writing.

WHY THE TEACHERLESS CLASS
HELPS MAKE WRITING BETTER

Probably the most helpful thing about the class is that you get many readings of your words, not just one. But if these readers don't know any more about writing than you do, how do they help you? They help you by being, in one sense worse readers, but in another sense better readers, than a regular teacher.

A teacher is usually too good a reader in the following ways. He usually reads and writes better than you do and knows more about the subject you are writing about. You are probably writing the thing because he asked you to, and, if it's an essay, he may well have picked a topic that he knows a lot about. If writing is an exercise in getting things into readers and not just onto paper, then usually it is too easy to get everything into the teacher's head. *Yet at the same time too hard to get anything in.* What I mean is that though he can usually understand everything you are trying to say (perhaps even better than you understand it); nevertheless he isn't really listening to you. He usually isn't in a position where he can be genuinely affected by your words. He doesn't expect your words actually to make a dent on him. He doesn't treat your words like real reading. He has to read them as an exercise. He can't hold himself ready to be affected unless he has an extremely rare, powerful openness.

So one of the genuinely valuable aspects of the reading you get from the teacherless class is that in a sense it is inferior: it will have "mistakes," the readers will miss some meanings that a teacher would get. The most obvious example is that

these readers give you better evidence of what is unclear in
your writing. They're not just telling you the places where
they think your writing is awkward because it doesn't conform to their idea of what good writing is. They are people
telling you where you actually confused them. A diverse
group of readers constitutes an ideal array of "channels" for
"sending your message across." You find out where there is
too much static or where the message is too weak. Sometimes
someone who knows very little about the subject is most useful here.

I have often seen the following process. Someone writes
something about a field he is expert in. He gets other experts
to read it. They understand it fine, at least they have no questions and seem to display no problems in understanding it. But
they don't like it very well, they are rather unpersuaded by it,
or somehow the writing doesn't affect them as the writer
thinks it should. He senses an importance in what he wrote
and they just don't seem to get it. But someone who *doesn't*
understand the matter at all shows the writer where the problem is: places where the idea is there, yes, and the expert readers felt they were understanding it, but really they weren't
hearing it as the writer intended it, weren't seeing it as the
writer was seeing it. They just read right through and said,
"uh huh, yes, I see," but if they had really seen it as the writer
saw it, they would have been forcibly struck.

Though the members of a teacherless class read, in a sense,
worse than a teacher, they also read better. They see your
writing every week. They hear you read things out loud.
They hear you react to other people's writing. They can
listen fully to your words—just listen and attend to their reactions—because they don't have to try to evaluate or give a

grade. They get to know your language, your way of handling words, so they can hear ideas, feelings, and nuances that are only partially encoded in the words. They hear the message behind the fog.

But how will it help you write better if they tell you that a message got across when "in the real world" it wouldn't have gotten across? I remember the evening when I first wrestled with this question. I was teaching an evening adult education class. I thought of my method as "hard nosed," "tough," "realistic." I was comfortable and in fact pleased with how useful it is for readers to be, as it were, *meaner* than a teacher would be to a piece of writing. But on this particular evening, three or four weeks into the course, the class was *nicer* than I would have been. There was a poem. People read it on paper. Everyone was left pretty cold. It clearly didn't work. But then someone asked the woman to read it out loud. Still nothing much. But the same reader asked her to read it once more—perhaps out of embarrassment at having nothing to say about the poem. And now people began to respond to it, hear things in it, finally be touched by it. It seemed to me these people weren't being hardnosed enough. I was sure it wasn't a very good poem, and reading it out loud didn't make it any better. They weren't supposed to like it like this. Here I thought I had a good empirical, real-world laboratory when now it looked as though perhaps I just had a too-easy, self-indulgent hot-house that will let people be too nice to each other.

I was very bothered but I still thought the class helped people, so I kept trying to figure out why. I came to a way of understanding the feedback process that I wouldn't otherwise have thought of.

This woman had written a poem—not a very good poem as

far as I could tell—but on that evening she had the main experience that makes people write more poems: her words got
through to the readers. She sent words out into the darkness
and heard someone shout back. This made her want to do it
again, and this is probably the most powerful thing that
makes people improve their writing. (It's not that the members of the class were "trying to say something nice." They
were actually getting an important meaning or experience
from the words. There is one sort of good teacher who always
seems to have something good to say about a student's writing. If you try to emulate this teacher's "technique" and always say something nice, it sounds false and doesn't seem to
work. His "technique" didn't consist of saying nice things but
rather of being such a good reader that he actually heard in
the words much of what the writer put in.)

You could describe the previous situation with the poem
by saying that the woman's "message" was all right (surely
there's no thought or feeling which wouldn't make a good
poem if transmitted in the right language); but there was too
much fog or static—she didn't have the right words; yet in the
end this audience finally got through the static to the message
itself and liked the poem.

But there's something wrong with describing the situation
this way. In the last analysis there is no such thing as static.
Human behavior, especially verbal behavior, is never random. We could only speak of static in a piece of writing if the
writer had St. Vitus's Dance and kept hitting random keys of
the typewriter, or splashed ink randomly across the page. Any
other weakness or mistake must be thought of as understandable if you only get to know this person's coding behavior.
Even completely mistaken uses of a word are understandable
to a listener who knows the speaker very well.

I'm not trying to say that writing which looks weak is really strong. I'm simply saying that all the weak, static-like, or fog-like elements in it are really decipherable, really meaningful, really messages. Most of them consist of too many and too conflicting messages which *function* as static because they are only half-coded and not in good order.

It is the human condition that when we emit words in speaking or writing, we are sending out lots and lots of messages. The reason why our word production is so unpowerful and ineffective is that we let all those messages mush in together and get in each other's way. What is rare is simply to send a message with no other conflicting messages. This explains that strange but crucial phenomenon in writing: someone writes something that is not original or earthshaking, writes it not elegantly and in a sense not even well, but somehow writes it with such directness and purity that it ends up hitting the reader with great force. He has finally managed to get rid of what *looks* like static, namely, all the half-coded, irrelevant messages, and all the undertones and overtones that get in the way of his utterance.

The idea that there's no such thing as static helps us understand how to improve a piece of writing: it does no good to say to someone, "get rid of the static here." He didn't write any static, he wrote nothing but messages. But he wasn't aware of most of those intruding or badly-coded messages. Take a simple example: a letter which asks for something but doesn't succeed in making it happen. The letter was understandable but it simply didn't work. A reader who doesn't know the writer at all could point out some mistakes and places where it might be clearer, but when asked why it didn't work would have to say, "I don't know. It's just not convincing." And if the receiver of the letter doesn't know the

writer, that is probably the only feedback he could give. But
readers who know the writer well and his ways of using and
responding to words can usually say much more. They will
be able to hear messages throughout, even though they are
faint: implications that the writer doesn't like the person he's
writing to, or fears him, or that he doesn't really expect his re-
quest to be granted, or doesn't really believe some of his own
reasons. These are not messages that the writer intended to
send. He will not be aware of them till he hears about them
from readers who know his coding habits well.

The important learning process here is that there is something you must *stop* doing—inhibit those intrusive messages—
but you can't stop doing something you are unaware of doing.
If someone is trying to stop tightening or clenching a muscle
he is unconsciously keeping tight, he must first experience
this tightening.[4]

So when a teacherless writing class gets going well, readers
don't just hear the writer's intended message behind the fog.
They also hear how the fog itself consists of unintended messages. The writer is persistently being told that there are implications in his words he didn't think he put there. When a
writer hears often enough that readers have such and such a
response, he finally has to suspect that perhaps the response is
appropriate. When he begins to acknowledge and then finally
to experience his sending of some message, he begins to be
able to stop sending it. *Or*—and this can be a very powerful
move toward better writing—he begins to be able to send it
louder and clearer.

4. The Alexander technique of kinesthetic training is based on this construc-
tive analysis of inhibition. See *The Resurrection of the Body: Selected Writings
of F. Matthias Alexander,* Edward Maisel, editor, New York, 1969.

PEOPLE LEARN FROM THE TRUTH
EVEN THOUGH THE TRUTH IS A MESS

People can't agree on a definition or specification of what goodness in writing consists of. Whenever anyone has a promising theory, it always leaves out some pieces of writing that most people agree are good, and includes some others they admit are bad. Even if you wanted to argue that there *is* a true theory of writing around but people are too stupid to agree about it, the fact remains that no one has been able to formulate this theory so that when you tell it to a talented person, it enables him to produce good writing.

Maybe this situation will change. I'm not a mystical skeptic. I believe any question has an answer, or else there is something the matter with the question; and if you change it in the right way, you can get an answer to this better question which completely satisfies your earlier misguided perplexity. But at the moment, writing is a black box: it is making marks on paper and then waiting to see what happens when other people come along and stare at those marks. Data. Evidence. And it is a mess. Not only do different people have different reactions. The same person is liable to have different reactions on different days. The reactions to a set of words are only partly a function of the words: they are also a function of the mood, temperament, and background of the reader, which are liable to be combined in shifting proportions from minute to minute.

Who would think a *learner* could learn from such a mess? It doesn't seem sensible. And so in the normal teaching situation, if the teacher has reactions to the student's words, he usually doesn't tell them accurately and honestly to the student because these reactions are unpredictable, temperamental, unprofessional, and usually unfair. He usually gives you a simpler story: he tells you what he thinks you did wrong and ought to do to make it right. Out of some kind of amalgam of his reactions and his working theory about good and bad writing, he somehow produces criticism and advice. The trouble is that his reaction is mostly hidden and his theory isn't true.

I am always noticing how much I can usually learn from someone with some strong obsession or axe to grind. If I get him to train his perceiving lens on something I've written, he almost always tells me more than the opposite kind of person who is notably judicious or moderate. There is liable to be a much higher proportion of distortion in the strong-lensed person, but there is also a much higher proportion of usable information. That information does not become usable by trying to pick through it and separate what's valid from what isn't. It's all a little distorted. I must hear it in conjunction with at least three or four different responses from three or four different strong-lensed people.

If someone has a hang-up about X and sees it in 50 per cent of what he reads (which is actually typical when you start learning someone's real reactions), then you better take him seriously when he sees X in what you wrote. He's an expert on X and can detect it in very small quantities. Very small quantities are important because they affect other readers who can't see X.

THE PROCESS OF LEARNING WRITING

Mathematics seems to be learnable one element at a time. It is possible—indeed they often say it is necessary—to stick to one element and master it before going on to the next. This means that you can see your progress. If you are not succeeding, you can find out with some accuracy where you went wrong.

The striking thing about learning to write is that people have been trying to teach it for as long as they've tried to teach mathematics yet no one has succeeded in making this kind of orderly, hierarchical progression that works. Someday someone may do it, but for the time being learning to write seems to mean learning contrasting but interdependent skills —double-binds: learning X and Y, but you can't do X till you can do Y, but you can't do Y till you can do X. (The proposition that it is theoretically impossible to learn to write has the ring of truth.)

From this model we can derive a learning curve that is remarkably like the shape of what it's really like to learn to write. There are long plateaus when you don't seem to make any progress at all. You are, in effect, wandering around in the underground activity of trying to get better at lots of different skills but always being at a disadvantage since you lack the other skills that are prerequisites. And even to the extent that you *make* progress and actually *do* come closer to being able to perform some of these skills—this progress is never *visible:* nothing budges till everything budges.

Long plateaus aren't the worst of it. There's also backsliding. You've been wandering around in the dark trying to get better at the interconnected, contrary skills, X, Y, and Z. Perhaps you've made some progress, though not yet visible or felt. But there inevitably comes a point in the learning process where you cannot get any better at XYZ till you start actually *using* them. And that means abandoning the global complex of interrelated skills you are now using, A, B, and

C. But since the skills are global and interrelated, and since you are now good at ABC, if you start using XYZ your writing will get much worse, in fact it will probably fall apart. That wouldn't happen in a hierarchical skill where you could really isolate elements and learn them one at a time.

Writing badly, then, is a crucial part of learning to write well. Indeed, regressing and falling apart are a crucial and usually necesary part of any complex learning.[5] Schools tend to emphasize success and thereby undermine learning. When the price of failure is very high, a learner tends to close himself off from improvement in this sort of complex, global skill. If he sticks with ABC, he can always turn out a better performance, a better product, a better grade, than if he embarks on XYZ.

If there is any validity in this model, it would explain why the most appropriate path for learning to write is *not* to try to break up the skill into its ideal progression of components which can be learned one at a time, but rather to try to set up some situation in which the learner can persevere in working at the whole skill in its global complexity. Since you have to work on all different aspects and there is no ideal order, you might as well feel free at any time to work on something different. Since it is going to require a lot of time, sweat, frustration, you might as well find some way of working that is enjoyable and rewarding in itself.

WHAT ABOUT GRAMMAR?

Just because there is usually right and wrong (or "standard" and "nonstandard") in matters like grammar, spelling, and punctuation, it doesn't mean that these matters do not bene-

5. See, for example, J. S. Bruner, *Studies in Cognitive Growth,* Wiley, 1966.

fit from the feedback of a teacherless class. For though this sort of class does not teach you the rules of grammar directly (I list some texts at the end of this book which will teach you these things), it will help make these matters less a problem. By learning the reactions of real readers, you will learn the effects of different mistakes. What sort of mistake is perceived? By which readers? Is this mistake felt to be important or trivial? Does it confuse the meaning? Does it annoy? distract? amuse? Does it make the reader consider the writer ignorant? lower-class? careless? superior? rude? The teacherless class will help you make a realistic decision about how well you would like to learn grammar—what level of correctness *you* want to attain in your writing. (Few writers avoid all mistakes in grammar. The publisher of this book, like almost every publisher, hires a professional to fix any mistakes in usage—or at least fix the ones I want fixed.)

If you decide you want special help in grammar, say so and everyone will go out of their way to look for errors. But don't let a concern about grammar hinder your efforts to improve your writing. Don't make a special effort on grammar until you are already comfortable and *much* more competent in your writing. In the meantime treat grammar as a matter of very late editorial correcting: never think about it *while you are writing*. Pretend you have an editor who will fix everything for you; then don't hire yourself for this job till the very end; and finally, for writing where grammar really matters, find someone good at it to catch the mistakes *you* miss. With this procedure you don't have to worry about it.

But some people feel you *cannot* become more competent in writing while you make bad mistakes in grammar. This isn't so. Consider an extreme case: a bunch of people who have a teacherless writing class who all make lots of grammatical mistakes. Perhaps they speak some other language and know English only partly, or perhaps they speak some "non-standard" dialect of English—or perhaps both. In any event, their normal speech is littered with what most speakers of the language would call terrible blunders. In all their writing for the teacherless class they will get *no* feedback on the basis of "good English."

They will probably develop some hybrid language that violates standard or correct English at every turn. (Or different members develop slightly different hybrids.) Where is the problem? Their writing will increase in clarity and power, like writing in any other "language" or "dialect." The hybrid will work fine for them. It will also work, though perhaps seem strange, for many people outside the group. When they want to write for an audience that insists on standard English, they must get someone to help them make the appropriate adjustments. And if they should want to get good at standard English themselves, it will be much easier when they are fluent writers and know what it is to wield some power with words, than when they are badly intimidated by the very attempt to write.

The idea that you cannot write competently unless you avoid mistakes in grammar is, I think, based on the feeling that writing with serious and extreme mistakes is incoherent. But when someone speaks any dialect, it is not incoherent even if it seems strange to speakers of a different dialect. *Real incoherence* comes when someone worries so much about lurking mistakes that he constantly stops and worries and changes direction in the middle of a phrase.

It's no accident that so much attention is paid to grammar in the teaching of writing. Grammar is the one part of writing that *can* be straightforwardly taught.

THE YOGURT MODEL

It may be hard to get a teacherless class going successfully—or any class whether or not it has a teacher—but if it does really get going it has a powerful momentum that helps keep it going. Almost every student and teacher has had the experience of being in a learning group that finally gets rolling. The group "takes off" and functions at a new and higher level. There is a great new force for learning and satisfaction: the members have learned to expect useful behavior and inhibit disruptive behavior in each other. The group has become a kind of self-regulating mechanism.

Therefore, any class which really achieves this take-off level should see in themselves a precious culture to be preserved. Yogurt. Not a class with an end, a "term." They should think of themselves as having created a living culture that can continue even when the membership has changed. (Or for those who don't like yogurt, a floating crap game.) Take advantage of the fact that different people will want to leave at different times. Some will stay briefly, some for a long time. Bring new members in gradually. Let them learn in the best way: looking over everyone's shoulder at a functioning enterprise and gradually moving into it. Just make sure that you always have your core of at least seven people committed to be there.

Compare this yogurt model with our current "movie" model of a learning structure. In the movie model, a course or class is a "show" with a fixed starting and stopping time, and it is played over and over again. Each term you start with a fresh group of people and no learning culture, and then at the end of twelve weeks or so, when a learning culture may be just getting going, you disband it, flush it down the toilet.

It wouldn't be hard to build the yogurt model into a university or school. (And indeed the Leicestershire or "open classroom" tends to imply the yogurt model.) Instead of defining groups by starting and stopping dates and by a subject matter that cannot change, define them by whether there is a learning culture. If a group has none, it is fine to disband it. But any group that has managed to create a culture should be asked not to let it die: if people want to leave and go on to something else, ask them to leave gradually so that new people can come in gradually. There will be different sorts of learning cultures. They can slowly change. The subject matter can slowly change. Membership (including teachers) can change. But the learning culture, which is probably the strongest aid in learning, would be preserved.

SUBJECTIVE BULLSHIT

Some people say, "Oh, this class is wonderful. At last it's a chance to stop being so impersonal and objective and rigorous. Here at last is a comfortable place. A place to relax." They've got it all wrong. Really the teacherless class asks you to be much more objective, impersonal, and rigorous than any conventional class. You must put your own responses out on the table, you must offer up your own reactions as pure data—not defend or justify or even discuss them—just reveal them and let the other person *use* them for his own private purposes.

Here's the speech I want to give to someone who thinks this class should be comfy; to someone giving me conventional feedback of only criticism and advice; to the members of a teacherless class I'm listening to on a tape when they talk too much about what good writing should consist of; and I especially want to give it to orthodoxy-bound teachers and intellectuals who call this class subjective and think they are tough and rigorous when really they are soft as soap because they don't dare think carefully about the nature of rigor and language:

Don't give me any more of that subjective bullshit. Don't ever tell me my writing is too unclear. Tell me what *you* were perceiving and how *you* were experiencing that passage you subjectively label unclear. Don't tell me I've got too many adjectives. That's subjective bullshit. There's no such thing as too many adjectives. There's great writing with twice as many adjectives. Tell me how *you* were reacting and what you were seeing and where. Don't talk to me about good writing and bad writing. No one knows. Don't give me a lot of untrustworthy nonsense. Give me some first-hand data I can trust, not a lot of second-hand conclusions based on hidden data and false hypotheses.

The appendix essay is my attempt to expand this speech in temperate language and reasoned argument.

MULTIPLE-CHOICE DIARY

Because there is no neat gradual way to learn to write and because progress *seems* so unpredictable and just plain slow, a major part of learning to write is learning to put up with this frustrating *process* itself. (This process accompanies any learning that involves the whole person rather than some discrete cognitive skill.)

I've tried below to make a start at erecting some of the

milestones in this boggy, inner landscape of learning. The list will give you an idea of some of the things you may expect. It will help you to realize you are progressing in the learning *process* even if improvement in writing itself is so unpredictable. I've listed them more or less as they came to mind. I know of no normal or preferable order. Perhaps you will miss many of these. Start your own diary; note others that are important for you.

_____a) Saw progress in my writing.

_____b) Got nowhere for four weeks. Endured. Didn't give up.

_____c) Gave up trying to write. Began again after five or six months.

_____d) This time really gave up. Didn't try again for a couple of years.

_____e) Tried the kind of writing I've always had a secret urge to do but had never dared try (that is, always wanted to write plays but had to write in a workshop for six weeks on more familiar kinds of writing before daring).

_____f) Wrote a long piece (not a freewriting) and had only one major bog-down—period of no progress, wheel-spinning, wanting to give up, falling apart. This means I only allowed one inning to the demons trying to stop me from writing.

_____g) Only gave them two innings.

_____h) One of the worst times writing—almost all wheel-spinning —right after one of the best.

_____i) Gave up writing a particular piece. Seriously thought I was giving it up for good. Something made me come back to it some time later and finish it. It was good.

j) Ditto, but it was terrible.

_____k) Almost finished something in which I thought I had definite point of view. Discovered I really had the opposite view. Reworked it and finished it.

_____l) Almost finished something. A small phrase caught my eye which had seemed merely a random detail, example, or flourish. Now seemed a bit more important. Developed it a bit. Before I finished, *it* was the real center of the piece; what I had previously considered the center was now relatively unimportant.

_____m) Brought the same piece back three or four times to the workshop in new versions. Almost obsessed with trying to get it right. Finally got it right.

_____n) Ditto, but never got it right.

_____o) Got a piece of feedback that seemed wierd and impossible. Later, something made me finally feel what he meant —finally got a real taste of what it was like for him to perceive my words: an entirely new perception of my words.

_____p) Actually enjoyed writing something.

_____q) Almost enjoyed writing something.

_____r) Almost enjoyed writing three pieces in a row.

_____s) Wrote something I thought great. Everyone else seemed to miss it; no one seemed to value it. Finally saw they were right.

_____t) Ditto, except that I could see that it was really good. Maybe not the best thing in the world, but much better than anything I had written and taking me a long way toward where I want to go. I could let their responses roll off my back and not be bothered at all.

_____u) Rewrote something on the basis of reactions and it came out very different. Much better.

_____v) Ditto, but much worse.

Freewritings:

_____a) Obsessed with idea of someone reading what I am writing. Made me almost incapable of producing words. A few meaningless words or phrases over and over again; or else things that seemed totally fake, untrue, deceptive.

_____b) Freewriting was fluent and easy; don't know why; what I produced seemed excellent. Only it didn't feel like *me* writing.

_____c) Ditto, but it did feel like me.

_____d) I could do nothing but the same sentence over and over

again. I knew it was stupid to write that way. Of course I
could have written other things. But I didn't want to. But
the sentence began to take on different meanings. By the
time I got near the end I was furious with rage. But for
some reason, at the very end I was calm and benign.

_____e) I couldn't stop talking to someone in my freewriting. But
I said things to him I didn't know I had on my mind and
by the end got to know him better.

_____f) Everything I wrote was untrue and fake. But what a
pleasure.

_____g) Near the beginning of the freewriting, I started produc-
ing words in a way that clearly was wonderful: they were
strong, clear, from my depths—both very good and very me.
But then it went away. I kept trying to recapture it—to
make it happen, to let it happen. To no avail.

Milestones as responder in class:

_____a) Gave reactions in a way that was new and difficult (that
is, used metaphors of clothing; made sounds).

_____b) Was left cold by a paper. No reaction at all. Said so.
Then 15 minutes later—or three days later—suddenly realized I had a very definite reaction I hadn't previously let
myself experience.

_____c) Had a reaction to a piece. Gave it. Later realized a very
different reaction was going on underneath (that is, I felt I
didn't like the piece but later realized that deep down I
liked it but was annoyed because it was trying for something
I didn't dare try for).

_____d) Had a definite response to every piece that class.

These process-oriented milestones may be useful and interesting but if you really care about your writing, you are
looking for milestones that mark substantive improvement in
your writing. If you spend some extra time and energy, you
can try to plot the improvement. In doing so you can learn a

great deal about yourself and about the skill of writing. What's needed is a kind of multiple-entry diary to accompany your use of the course.

Each week, take a fresh sheet of paper and write a brief account of what you think you got out of that week's work: free-writing for class, any other writing, and class reactions. These entries cannot profess to *the truth*. They are meant as a record of how you see things at the moment.

Then every six weeks or so, go back and read over these diary-entries and some of that week's writing. See if you can now see things better. What improvement do you find over the whole period? Any changes or patterns? In particular, see if you can see what was going on during any long, seemingly dry spells when you didn't seem to get anywhere: can you now sense what was being learned underground during this period when the surface was unchanged? Try looking at it as a period in which you were struggling, as it were, to *unlearn* something. During this period you were learning from the reactions of others that there was some basic habit in your manner of generating words that made them backfire or fail to get through to readers; perhaps some basic habit in your *stance* toward an audience (such as arrogance or fear); but it was a period in which you were virtually stuck, because you had nothing to replace it with; or you were used to it and uncomfortable without it. Such changes usually cannot be clearly seen at the time. But they are the only ones that really make a profound improvement in your writing. Since they take so long and are often largely underground, you may not be able to see them till your second or third retrospective view.

If you decide something was going on in a particular week which you had been unable to perceive at the time, note it now on that week's diary sheet, along with the date of this new comment. You may have yet another and different comment in the future. Revise history.

It can help you see your present writing better if you fish out pieces of your writing from before you started the course: a year ago, three years ago, ten years ago.

The Doubting Game and the Believing Game— An Analysis of the Intellectual Enterprise

"I can't believe that," said Alice.

"Can't you?" the Queen said in a pitying tone. "Try again; draw a long breath, and shut your eyes."

Alice laughed. "There's no use trying," she said; "one can't *believe impossible things."*

"I dare say you haven't had much practice," said the Queen. "When I was your age I always did it for half an hour a day. Why, sometimes I've believed as many as six impossible things before breakfast. . . ."

Through the Looking Glass
LEWIS CARROLL

WHEN people first encounter the teacherless writing class, they often call it anti-intellectual. To academics especially, the idea of listening to everyone else's reading no matter what it is, refraining from arguing, and in fact trying to *believe* it, seems heretical and self-indulgent.

Many intelligent people would dismiss the charge: "Intellectual schmintellectual! Who cares?" The trouble is I care. I think of myself as an intellectual. And besides, the charge of anti-intellectuality has been leveled at me so many times over the last few years that I want to try to answer it at length.

In what follows I attempt to justify many of the practices and ways of thinking I have come to, both in the teacherless writing class and in many other activities. It is heavily theoretical not just because many attacks are on that level but because I value theory. The preceding chapters of this book can be understood and used by themselves—without this more general final argument.

The charge of anti-intellectualism comes from a faulty understanding of the intellectual enterprise. An intellectual is someone who tries to figure out what is true by means of the best processes available, and uses them in a rational, disciplined way to try to avoid deluding himself. The basic processes in the teacherless writing classes are central to the intellectual enterprise.

As a way of beginning the argument, consider a general situation of looking for the truth: you have a pile of conflicting assertions about some matter and you want to know which are true. There are two basic games you can use, the doubting game and the believing game.

The doubting game seeks truth by indirection—by seeking error. Doubting an assertion is the best way to find the error in it. You must assume it is untrue if you want to find its weakness. The truer it seems, the harder you have to doubt it. *Non credo ut intelligam:* in order to understand what's wrong, I must doubt.

To doubt well, it helps if you make a special effort to extricate yourself from the assertions in question—especially those which you find self-evident. You must hold off to one side the self, its wishes, preconceptions, experiences, and commitments. (The machinery of symbolic logic helps people do this.) Also, it helps to run the assertion through logical transformations so as to reveal premises and necessary consequences and thereby flush out into the open any hidden errors. You can also doubt better by getting the assertions to battle each other and thus do some of the work: They are in a relationship of conflict, and by getting them to wrestle each other, you can utilize some of *their* energy and cleverness for ferreting out weaknesses.

The believing game also proceeds by indirection. Believe *all* the assertions. (If you merely look through the pile and pick out what seems truest, that would be the guessing game or the intuition game, not the believing game. Guessing has its own special power but I won't be exploring it here.[6]

6. See my essay, "Real Learning" in the *Journal of General Education*, XXIII, #2, July, 1971.

In the believing game the first rule is to refrain from doubting the assertions, and for this reason you take them one at a time and in each case try to put the others out of your head. You don't want them to fight each other. This is not the adversary method.

In the believing game we return to Tertullian's original formulation: *credo ut intelligam:* I believe in order to understand. We are trying to find not errors but truths, and for this it helps to believe. It is sometimes impractical to give to some assertions the fullest sort of belief: commitment and action. But there is a kind of belief—serious, powerful, and a genuine giving of the self—that it is possible to give even to hateful or absurd assertions. To do this requires great energy, attention, and even a *kind* of inner commitment. It helps to think of it as trying to get inside the head of someone who saw things this way. Perhaps even constructing such a person for yourself. Try to have the experience of someone who made this assertion.

To do this you must make, not an act of self-extrication, but an act of self-insertion, self-involvement—an act of projection. And similarly, you are helped in this process, not by making logical transformations of the assertion, but by making metaphorical extensions, analogies, associations. This helps you find potential perceptions and experiences in the assertion—helps you get a toehold so you can climb inside and walk around.

These then, in thumbnail form, are the two games that occupy this chapter. They could be called different names to bring out different characteristics. The doubting game could be called the self-extrication game, the logic game, or the dialectic of propositions. The believing game could be called the involvement or self-insertion game, the metaphor game, or the dialectic of experience.

THE MONOPOLY OF THE DOUBTING GAME

In a sense this essay is an extended attack on the doubting game. But I make this attack as someone who himself values the doubting game and is committed to it. Indeed I attempt to make my argument persuasive to someone who accepts only the doubting game. My goal is only to make the doubting game move over and grant a legitimacy to the believing game.

For somehow the doubting game has gained a monopoly on legitimacy in our culture. I'm not quite sure how. I see in Socrates this tendency to identify the intellectual process with the doubting game. I think this is the reason why his "voice" had a vocabulary of only one word, "no." Socrates believed a lot of things, but he seemed to have an overriding commitment to logic—what he called "reason." The essential quality of the Socratic dialogues is reductive and deflating: some belief is shown to be silly or empty or contradictory. Occasionally he tried to affirm something by logic (for example, the existence of the soul after death), but usually when affirming, he relinquished the doubting game and logical dialectic, and turned to myth, metaphor, and allegory.

Descartes gave us the name "doubting" or "skepticism" for our method. He felt the way to proceed to the truth was to doubt everything. This spirit has remained the central tradition in western civilization's notion of the rational process. Socrates said the unexamined life is not worth living. Descartes said, in effect, that the undoubted thought is not worth entertaining.

Perhaps the doubting game gets some of its monopoly through the success of natural science since the seventeenth century. There seems to be a skeptical ideology to science. Scientists pride themselves on not being gullible, not believing things easily. Some scientists talk as though they never really believe anything at all, but merely *act as though* certain things were true if they haven't yet been disproved. In this view, the experimental method is nothing but the attempt to disprove things.[7]

7. For the view that science is nothing but the organized enterprise of trying to disprove—associated with the name Carl Popper—see two very lucid books by the Nobel Prize winner, Peter Medawar, *Induction and Intuition in Scientific Thought* (The Jayne Lectures, 1968), and *The Art of the Soluble* (London, 1967). For the competing view of science which insists that it operates by affirming propositions, not just disconfirming them, see Carl Hempel, *The Philosophy of the Natural Sciences*.

However it happened, we now have a state of affairs where to almost anyone in the academic or intellectual world, it seems as though when he plays the doubting game he is being rigorous, disciplined, rational, and tough-minded. And if for any reason he *refrains* from playing the doubting game, he feels he is being un-intellectual, irrational, and sloppy. Even those few people who are actually against the doubting game nevertheless give in to the same view of the intellectual enterprise: they assume they must be against intellectuality and rationality itself if they are against the doubting game.

This is the trap that results from the monopoly of the doubting game. In the next few sections I will fight that trap by trying to show that there is a definite truth about the meaning of words; that the doubting game doesn't help us know this truth; but that the believing game does.

THE TRUTH ABOUT MEANING AND WORDS

In this section I wish to demonstrate that when someone says "this set of words means such and such," he is either correct or incorrect. His assertion is either true or false. (There is also a border-line situation which I will clarify.)

My account of meaning is grounded in what real people do when they speak and write. When people speak or write success-fully with each other it looks as though there is a transfer of mean-ing: the speaker puts the meaning *into the words* and the listener *takes it out* at the other end. If you look at it from the larger per-spective this account is fair: the listener ends up knowing what the speaker wanted him to know and ends up knowing something he never knew before, and so it must be that the words put this knowledge into his head. But it is important also to take a closer perspective and realize that, strictly speaking, words cannot *con-tain* meaning. Only people have meaning. Words can only have meaning *attributed to them by people*. The listener can never get any meaning out of a word that he didn't put in. Language can only consist of a set of directions for building meanings *out of one's own head*. Though the listener's knowledge seems new, it is also not new: the meaning may be thought of as *structures* he never had in his head before, but *he* had to build these new structures out of ingredients *he* already had. The speaker's words were a set of directions for assembling this already-present material.

To change the metaphor. Meaning is like movies inside the head. I've got movies in my head. I want to put them inside yours. Only I can't do that because our heads are opaque. All I can do is try to be clever about sending you a sound track and hope I've done it in such a way as to make you construct the right movies in your head. What's worse, of course, is that since neither of us can see the movies in each other's head, we are apt to be mistaken about how well we are doing in trying to make the other person show himself the movie we have in mind.

We can let ourselves talk about words "having meaning" and even "carrying meaning from one head to another" as long as we now realize these phrases denote something complex: the words don't transport the contents of my head into yours, they give you a set of directions for building your own meaning. If we are both good at writing directions and following directions for building meaning, we end up with similar things in our heads—that is, we communicate. Otherwise, we experience each other's words as "not having any meaning in them," or "having the wrong meaning in them."

The question is then how these meaning-building rules operate in ordinary language. Meaning in ordinary language—English, for example—is midway on a continuum between meaning in dreams and meaning in mathematics.

Dreams may be hard to interpret, but the nature of the meaning situation is very simple because there is no audience. Dreams are all "speaking" and no "listening": dreams are for the sake of dreaming, not for the sake of interpreting. Therefore, though dreams or dream-images *have* particular, definite meanings, they *can* mean anything. They have whatever meaning the dreamer of that particular dream built into them. The rules for dreaming are as follows: let anything mean anything. (We could be fancy and say that the meaning-building rules for dreams are the rules of "resemblance" and "association." But everything resembles everything else to some extent, and anything is liable to be associated somehow with anything else. Thus anything can mean anything.) If we dream of a gun or a steeple, we may be talking about a penis, but then again we may not. And we may dream about a penis with any image at all. In dreaming you can never make a mistake.

At the other extreme is a language like mathematics. Here people have gone to the trouble to nail down the rules for building meaning into symbols. Something may mean *only* what these publicly acknowledged rules allow it to mean. In mathematics there *are* mistakes, and any argument about what something means or whether there is a mistake can be settled without doubt or ambiguity. (Perhaps there are exceptions in some advanced mathematical research.)

Meaning in ordinary language is in the middle. It is pushed and pulled simultaneously by forces that try to make it fluid and dreamlike but also fixed like mathematics.

The individual user of ordinary language is like the dreamer. He is apt to build in any old meaning to any old word. Everybody has just as many connotations and associations to a word as he does to an image. Thus, as far as the individual is concerned, a word is liable—and often tends—to mean absolutely anything.

To illustrate this dream-like fluidity of ordinary language, notice that words *do* in fact end up meaning anything as they move through time and across mountain ranges. "Down" used to mean "hill" ("dune"), but because people said "down hill" a lot ("off-dune"), and because they were lazy ("adown"), finally hill means down. Philology, it has been said, is a study in which consonants count for very little and vowels for nothing at all. A word may change its meaning to absolutely anything.

But the mathematics-like force for order is just as strong. That is, though words in ordinary language *can* mean anything, they only *do* mean what the speech community lets them mean at that moment. But unlike the case of mathematics, these agreements are not explicitly set down and agreed to. That is, our rules for building meaning into words are unspoken and are learned by doing, by listening to others, and even by listening to ourselves. It's like one of those party games where people get you to start playing before you know the rules of the game and indeed part of the fun is learning gradually to understand the rules *after* you find yourself following them. When you pick up the rules you can play—you can send and receive messages with others who know the rules. These rules for building meaning may be thought to be written down in dictionaries. But dictionaries are only records of yesterday's rules, and today's may be somewhat different. And dictionaries don't tell all the meanings that speakers send to each other in words.[8]

The dynamism between the dream characteristics and the math characteristics in ordinary language is important: there is a constant tug of war. The individual is tending to allow words to mean anything—just as he allows dream images to mean whatever he builds in. Not because he is naughty but simply because he is a meaning-building creature and cannot refrain from constantly building new meanings into everything he encounters.

But the speech community is constantly curbing this looseness. When an individual speaker means things by a set of words which the community of listeners does not "hear," he tends to give in to the community and stop meaning those things by those words: that is, when they don't build in at their end what he builds in at his, he either stops building it in or else remains unconscious of building it in. In either case, he no longer treats these as real

8. See, for example, C. E. Osgood, *The Measurement of Meaning*, Urbana, 1957.

meanings of the words. Similarly, when an individual listener hears things in a set of words which the community of speakers do not mean, he also tends to give in to the community and stop hearing those meanings or stop being aware of having those meanings for those words. (The exceptions to this process illustrate it well. When there are listeners who are especially eager to know what is on someone's mind—someone like a specially loved child or a poet such as Blake—they will learn to interpret his words even if he talks like a dreamer. If there's enough utterance and enough care, the code can always be cracked.)

The history of meaning in a language is the history of this power struggle between dream characteristics and math characteristics. Rules for meaning-building change when some speaker is somehow powerful and makes people "hear" in an utterance what they never used to hear in it. And even a listener can be powerful in this subtle way (be an unmoved mover) and make people "mean" in an utterance what they had not meant before. When, on the other hand, the community holds its own, meanings don't change. Humpty Dumpty put his finger on it:

"But 'glory' doesn't mean 'a nice knockdown argument,' " Alice objected.

"When *I* use a word," Humpty Dumpty said in a rather scornful tone, "it means just what I choose it to mean—neither more nor less."

"The question is," said Alice, "whether you *can* make words mean so many different things."

"The question is," said Humpty Dumpty, "who is to be master that's all."

Through the Looking Glass
LEWIS CARROLL

The picture is oversimplified, however, if we talk of only *one* speech community. For actually there are many overlapping speech communities for each individual—building up to the largest one: all speakers of, say, English. Smaller subcommunities are in the middle in this power struggle. On the one hand, they exert stabilizing force upon the individual's dreamlike fluid tendency of meaning. But on the other hand, they are not as strongly stabilizing as the larger speech community is—that is, I can change the meaning-building rules of my friends sooner than I can do it to a larger community. And so, in fact, the smaller communities turn out to act as forces for *fluidity* upon larger communities.

This model implies that meaning in ordinary language consists of delicate, flexible transactions among people in overlapping speech communities—peculiar transactions governed by unspoken agreements to abide by unspecified, constantly changing rules as to what meanings to build into what words and phrases. All the parties merely keep on making these transactions and assuming that all the other parties abide by the same rules and agreements. Thus, though words are capable of extreme precision among good players, they nevertheless float and drift all the time.

I can now give a clear picture of what I meant by speaking of the *truth* about the meaning of an utterance—the correct reading of a text: that interpretation is correct which the speech community builds into those words. We have a borderline case if an interpretation fits some speech communities and not others, for example, a reading which fits sixteenth-century usage and not present-day usage, or which fits slang and doesn't fit standard English.

This model confirms the commonsense but confusing notion that sometimes an individual maverick reading is true and sometimes it is false. For it is natural, as we have seen, for every individual to have a more dream-like meaning for a set of words than what the speech community has tacitly agreed to. Such an interpretation, thus, is usually false: it's ok for dreaming, but our notion of meaning in ordinary language involves a community and communication. But an individual *may* come up with a reading of a text which, though no one in the community has ever thought of it, nevertheless conforms to that community's rules. Such a reading is correct, even though no one in the community ever thought of it before. The ideal test is this: tell the reading to the community, and it is correct if they say, "Of course! Yes! We never thought of that interpretation, but now that you point it out, clearly it is right. We see that it grows out of our rules for meaning." If they say "Huh?" or "Nonsense!" ideally that is a sign of an incorrect reading. But in reality it *may* still be a correct reading and conform to the rules of the community, but those particular people were too unskillful to see it because it was a difficult reading and perhaps a hard text. So we can summarize as follows: that reading is correct which the speech community builds in or *could build in* without violating its rules.

This model also permits us to cut through the difficulties that usually surround discussions about whether a text has more than one correct reading. When people talk of more than one correct reading they are usually falling into—or persuaded they are falling into—the implication that any reading is as correct as any other. But here we can see that a text can have more than one correct reading if those readings conform to the meaning-building rules of the speech community; and yet *other* readings are still clearly incorrect.

There is a simple reason for the possibility of more than one meaning in one utterance, and again it derives from the facts of how real people use words. It stems from the tendency to economize energy. If I am making three motions to do three tasks and there is a way for me to get the three tasks done in one motion, I will drift into that economy if I can. It simply turns out that you can send more than one message with only one utterance. Save on postage. People naturally do this. It is possible with one set of words to make someone show two different movies in his head—or to make two different people show different movies to themselves. Let me repeat: this does not undo the previous analysis of correct interpreting. These two movies are not any old movies, they are only those movies permitted by the speech community's rules. It's just that those rules—because of flexibility and redundancy—permit an utterance to result in two legal movies, not just one. Other movies are still illegal.

SHORT DIGRESSION ON THE NEW CRITICS

The New Critics were after the real thing: they wanted the real truth about the meaning of a text. I think they were right to want it. I want it. To get it, however, I feel I must violate some of their practices—practices which became misleadingly sanctified. But I have a strong sense of seeking their goal and working in their tradition.

The main thing they did to advance the search for the real truth about meaning was to try to make the question empirical rather than *a priori*. They took it out of the hands of special people who were felt to have a monopoly on deciding what a text meant: the author and the scholar. They insisted rightly that the author might be wrong about what his text meant. And they were also right to insist that the scholar must not pronounce what a text means on the basis of his study of the author's themes or the period's *zeitgeist*—must not pronounce what the text *ought* to mean.

They won this battle by locating meaning in the text and showing persuasively how the author or the scholar could be wrong about meaning. But they made the mistake of locating meaning *exclusively* in the text: in their fear of baloney and their itch for high standards, they couldn't bear to go back inside the author's head or to look inside the heads of real readers. (I. A. Richards took a peek and merely shuddered.) It's true that it would be nice to avoid getting into these messy places, but meanings *do* depend on events in the consciousnesses of the speech community. The rules for meaning are constantly drifting through communities and time.

There was another way which their desire for a toughminded truth made them insist on a tidier truth than the reality of words allows. They assumed that the meaning of a set of words was single. Yet since they were the best readers around and very smart too, they usually discovered many or all the correct meanings of a text. This is why they fell into the habit of seeing irony, tension, and contradiction almost everywhere. Sometimes the irony and contradiction are really there. But sometimes, though all the elements of the readings are correct, they are simply different, non-ironic messages carried in one utterance-envelope, not parts of a single complex message.

But even in this tendency, there is something to recommend their weakness for irony. For they were considering mostly works of art and I think it is reasonable (though not essential) to consider a work of art as characterized by coherence among elements. By assuming that the artist was successful—that all the meanings do in fact cohere—you improve your chances of finding elusive coherences that are really there. The New Critics found a lot of good ones. But too much haste to find coherence produces the characteristic shortcoming of new critical reading: a lack of tolerance for readings that *don't* seem to cohere—especially maverick readings and naïve readings of strong simple feelings. If you want to find the coherence that is really there, you must assume as a working hypothesis that it is there. But first you must find all the meanings that are there, and to do this, it helps to assume as a working hypothesis that all perceived meanings are really there too, however incoherent. New Critics don't have enough tolerance for *in*coherence and *lack* of irony.

WHY THE DOUBTING GAME DOESN'T WORK WITH ASSERTIONS OF MEANING

So there is a real truth about the meaning of an utterance or a text—a hard, commonsense, empirical truth: that reading is correct which the speech community builds in or *could build in* without violating its rules.

But the doubting game will not help us locate it. Though a critic may make an incorrect assertion about the meaning of a poem, though a student may make an incorrect assertion about the meaning of a book, though I may make an incorrect assertion about the meaning of an utterance, the doubting game is powerless to demonstrate our error. There are no rules for identifying false assertions of meaning. Whenever anyone ascribes a meaning to an utterance, it is always a waste of time to argue against him. Negative arguments cut no ice.

You may say, for example, that the meaning I propose is internally self-contradictory. But the meaning in the utterance may indeed be self-contradictory, and I may have interpreted the text just right. You may say that my reading contradicts such and such a meaning that we know or have good reason to believe is a correct meaning. But the utterance may contain these two contradictory meanings and thus both readings are correct. You may say that my reading contradicts what appears in the third stanza. But my reading may be relatively absent from Stanza III and the other correct reading more dominant there. You may say that my reading depends on taking "black" to mean "white" which is opposite to what it really means. But in fact black may also imply white here—only faintly, and depending on a context built up in accordance to the community's meaning-building rules. You may say that my reading is contradictory to everything else the writer wrote or everything characteristic of the period. But this meaning may be something new and uncharacteristic—and it certainly need not have been conscious on the part of the writer. You may say that I refuse to give any supporting evidence for my reading. Now here you may consider this sufficient grounds for not wanting to listen to me, but it doesn't make my reading any more apt to be wrong. I may have found a meaning that is genuinely in the text which neither you nor anyone else could hear—that is, a meaning which is "legal" or conforms to the speech community's rules for building in meaning but which for some reason is hard for most members of that community to build in. Most often this is a meaning which is not only difficult and faint, but also contrary to more prominent meanings in the text. And it may be so difficult for me to hear and go so much against the grain of my thinking that I cannot put my finger on the evidence that makes me hear that reading.

On the other hand, of course, in any of these cases, I *may* be dead wrong.

The fact is that negative argument—the doubting game—requires logic and evidence, and here they don't work. No discovery of dissonance or contradiction shows that any reading is less likely to be correct.

This state of affairs violates current practice and discourse, but actually it is in line with common sense. For only "humble" assertions of meaning have this invulnerability to the doubting game—not "pushy" or exclusive ones. If I say, "It *doesn't* mean X, it means Y," you are right to scoff: my denial of X cuts no ice. But if I restrict myself to saying, "It means Y; I don't know about X," I cannot be usefully argued against.

It may be thought that I am just talking about special fringes of meaning that only occur in literature. It's true that the study of literature requires attending to as many correct meanings in a text as possible: many works of literature don't achieve coherence —or even meaningfulness—till you attend to fainter meanings along with more obvious ones. But these same kinds of faint meanings operate in everyday speech. The contribution of psychiatry has been to show us how well we all attend to meanings that may be very "faint" and "symbolic" or literary.

So at last we can understand a disconcerting reality of life: you can never win an argument against an English teacher or a psychiatrist. There are no rules for showing that an assertion of meaning is false. This explains why, in such a realm, arguments are so often settled by matters like who has the greater authority, who is getting paid, who can in some sense shout loudest, or what kinds of answers happen to be in fashion. This explains why people who are in the habit of playing the doubting game rigorously —scientists and positivists—feel that when they come to a realm like this they are in the realm of nonsense or complete relativism where there is no such thing as truth.

THE BELIEVING MUSCLE

The monopoly of the doubting game makes people think the doubting muscle—the sensitivity to dissonance—is the only muscle in their heads, and that belief is nothing but the absence of doubt: the activity of believing something consists of refraining from doubting it; or better yet, trying to doubt it but not succeeding.

But there is a believing muscle and it is different. It puts the self into something. The way it gets at the truth is illustrated by the following common occurrence in visual perception. We look off into the distance and see an animal in a field but we don't know what it is. It looks as though it might be a horse or a dog. Perhaps our list of alternatives is longer. But we have no special knowledge to draw on (such as whose field it is) and there is no other object nearby that settles the matter for us. Yet within 30 seconds or so we *do* know it is a dog and not a horse. What happened? Where did our knowledge come from?

In most cases it did not come from a negative testing such as, for instance, holding up some kind of picture of horse and finding dissonance or contradiction. This is possible in some cases, of course: check it out for tail-behavior, perhaps. But not what we usually do. In most cases it is a matter of trying to "believe"—in this case "see"—both dog and horse and doing better with dog. We don't disprove horse, we affirm dog. We try to put ourselves into the object as horse and as dog, and we get ourselves further into it as dog. Subjectively, this is the experience of having it appear sharper as dog. When we try to see it as horse, it stays blurrier. I think we could say that we get more visual information when we consider it as dog than when we do as horse. We see *more* dog than horse.

By believing an assertion we can get farther and farther into it, see more and more things in terms of it or "through" it, use it as a hypothesis to climb higher and higher to a point from which more can be seen and understood—and finally get to the point where we can be more sure (sometimes completely sure) it is true. This was only possible by inhibiting the doubting game: if we had started doubting we would have found so many holes or silly premises we would have abandoned it. Only by getting far enough into it could we get to the point where there was sufficient evidence and understanding to show that it was indeed true, and this was only possible by believing it.

Imagine the paradigm use of the believing game to find the correct reading of a text: you believe the text means X; someone else believes it means Y; as it happens, you are wrong and he is right, but of course neither of you can know that at first. The question is how you get to the truth and abandon your error? If you engaged in the doubting game, neither person's argument would get anywhere. The "power of your arguments" would simply reflect each person's rhetorical skill and have nothing to do with the truth. At some level, both of you would probably realize this and stubbornly stick to your guns. And so it would go till weariness, fashion, or authority had its way.

The only way you can know that X is wrong is if you do in fact *try* as hard as you can to believe Y. If you are good at believing, you will at some point be able to see or feel that Y is truer. It will be just like the dog and the horse. You will be able to see more of the text with Y and see it more coherently and sharply.

This then is the leverage of the believing muscle: believing two things and thereby being able to have a trustworthy sense that one is better than the other. But there is no leverage—no increased trustworthiness—unless *both* are believed. This can be illustrated by considering the paradigm situation again, but this time put yourself in what turns out to be the trickier position: *you* start out with the right answer—you believe Y. But of course you don't know you're right. The question this time is how you can attain any trustworthy knowledge that Y is true. Your only strategy is to try to reproduce the previous paradigm situation of leverage. Your belief in Y will become more trustworthy only if you can get *yourself* to really believe X. If you can really do that and come back to Y and find Y better again, then at last you have attained leverage. Your knowledge of Y is at last much more trustworthy.

In performing this strange little dance with yourself, you have played the believing game. People with good judgment in areas like literature where disproof is impossible—people who simply turn out to be right in their judgment more often than most of us do—are distinguished, I would assert, by being especially good believers, especially good solitary players of the believing game. They attain more truth because they can believe more things than most of us can. And believe them *better—really* believe them: for in the ceremony just described, if you were only half-hearted in your attempt to believe X—if you were just doing it to bolster your belief in Y—then you might have missed any truth in X. For X *might* in fact have been true and Y false, and so you would have erroneously believed Y because you weren't good enough at believing.

There are people who are particularly good at the doubting game—who can always sense a contradiction or lapse in logic even if it is very hidden. It would seem that they have a very fine, very highly developed doubting muscle. We see the same thing with the believing game: some individuals are particularly good at being many people, being a chameleon, seeing the truth in very different and contradictory propositions or perceptions, making metaphors and building novel models.

Perhaps the difference in the two games comes from the fact that the doubting game deals with classes of things (for example, all Xs) whereas the believing game deals with particular, unique things (for example, this particular utterance, which is not the same as any other). When you are working with universal propositions (all Xs are Y), you have only one useful button to push: disconfirm. The only trustworthy thing you can do to a universal proposition, the only thing you can do which increases your knowledge about whether it is true or false, is to try to disprove it. But when you are working with an assertion of meaning, a particular unique thing, it's only the other button that does you any good: affirm. The only trustworthy thing you can do to such an assertion, the only thing you can do to increase your knowledge of whether such and such a meaning really *is* in the text is to try to share that perception, try to have that experience of meaning.

The cornerstone of the believing game is the principle that whatever your mistake may be, your only chance of correcting it is by affirming, believing, not-arguing. Your two possible mistakes are blindness or projection. If you are blind—that is, if you fail to see a meaning that is there—obviously your only cure is to go around trying to believe assertions of meaning till you finally come to see the meaning you have been blind to.

If you are projecting—if you are seeing a meaning that isn't really there—your only hope is *also* to go around trying to believe other assertions of meaning till you attain a better view of the text and stop having your hallucination. It is not foolproof, of course. But the affirmatory process is your only hope. A superior understanding of a text usually does in fact relieve you of your mirage.

I think this model of the believing game gives us a better view of the real world of literary criticism. On the one hand, we can understand its characteristic shortcomings: people either stick to their interpretations come hell or high water, or else they change their minds on the basis of what's in fashion or who has greater status. But on the other hand, criticism is not always arbitrary, and when a group of readers agrees that X is a better reading than Y, they are sometimes correct. They have played the believing game though they were usually hindered by arguing. In the case of X, they have tried to agree with it, go into it, see with it, and all have been struck with its fruitfulness. As in seeing the dog, the more they looked at the text as X, the more details and coherence they saw. In the case of Y, they tried in good faith as hard as they could to agree with it, go into it, see with it, but they find the effort less fruitful. As in looking at the "horse," it stays fuzzy.

The function of a good critic, then, is not to discredit a bad reading but to make better readings more available. A good reading is like a good lens. You don't so much see "it" as see through it to more of the text. Incorrect readings are never disproven or even undermined. They merely fall into disuse because they don't "resolve" the text so well.

MEANING-MAKING AS GESTALT-MAKING

I wish to widen my net. Up till now I have been speaking only of meanings in words. As though it were only a peculiarity of *words* that makes wrong interpretations impossible to argue against. As though the doubting game breaks down and the believing game is required only in the case of assertions of meaning. But I think everything I am saying applies also to most procedures in the humanities and social sciences (and even in disputes between what Thomas Kuhn[9] calls paradigms in natural science).

To illustrate the believing game I used an example from vision: seeing the dog/horse. Someone might object that finding the meaning in a set of words and trying to see an animal in the distance are very different. But both are examples of finding or making a gestalt.

9. *The Structure of Scientific Revolutions,* Chicago, 1962.

A gestalt is the form, shape, or organization that we find in something—say a picture or a view—that permits us to see it as coherent instead of just disconnected, buzzing, blooming marks. Optical illusions illustrate the phenomenon of gestalt-building: for example, there is the line drawing that looks like a chalice if you look at it one way but looks like the profiles of two men facing each other if you look at it differently. But it doesn't look like both at once. It jumps and looks very different as you change gestalts. Here is a visual field, then, that invites two conflicting gestalts.

The making or seeing of a gestalt is central to vision. It was the contribution of gestalt psychologists to show that we tend to see coherence not only in normal views or pictures, but even when we are looking at something broken or disconnected. Visual mistakes *add* coherence as often as they take it away. The act of seeing seems inherently an act of construction that makes wholes out of fragments.[10] The same thing goes on in sound: we hear as melody and shape what are disconnected sounds.[11]

The same thing goes on in finding meaning in a set of words. Because words are full of redundancy and ambiguity (which turns out to be efficient in a communicating medium) an utterance tends to consist, as it were, of seventeen words, each capable of as many as three or four meanings. In listening, you've got to hold up in the air countless possible meanings of parts—and even

10. See Ulrich Neisser, *Cognitive Psychology,* New York, 1967.
11. See Victor Zuckerkandl, *Sound and Symbol,* Princeton, 1956.

meanings of the whole—and then find the whole that makes the most sense. Reading or listening is like seeing: you have to build the gestalt that makes the most coherence out of an ambiguous semantic field. Building meaning into a set of words then is a subset of the universal human activity of gestalt-making. Finding explanations for a set of data is another subset.

The doubting game would work in gestalt-making or explanation-making *only* if you adopt two special rules: 1. *only one* gestalt or *only one* explanation is allowed and it must use *all* the data; 2. no correct gestalt or explanation may contradict another. If you adopt these rules the law of contradiction works: you can disprove or falsify a gestalt or explanation by showing it doesn't use some piece of the data or because it contradicts some other correct one.

But I don't think we have to adopt these special rules. I don't think we use them in trying to deal with the physical world or even in trying to read a work of literature. Few sets of data are *all* explained by one explanation; few fields are restricted to one gestalt.

THE MYTH OF THE LABORATORY RATS

Where Plato proposes the myth of the cave as an image of man's life, I propose the myth of the experimental psychology laboratory. We are like rats who have been taught to see rectangles and circles. But what happens when they show us an ellipse? If it is a long pointy ellipse we see a rectangle. If it is a round, mild ellipse, we see a circle. Ellipses we don't see. Ellipses don't exist for us. Here is is a myth that helps us see what the physicists do when they talk about light as a "wave/particle": though they haven't invented the ellipse yet, at least they have the sense to call what they are looking at a circle/rectangle.

What should give us pause is the fact that the reason physicists have the sense to do this is not because they are so much smarter than literary critics or political scientists but because they are operating in a realm where the doubting game works better: they can get their perceptions of light into disprovable propositions (or at least propositions more disprovable than in literature) so they know they aren't looking at *just* a rectangle or *just* a circle —light isn't *just* a wave or *just* a particle. They can get the law of contradiction to work for them and force them to invent this piece of novelty, the wave/particle. There is hope that if they keep at it they will finally "invent" the ellipse they have been looking at all along.

But for literary critics or political scientists, argument about whether they are looking at a rectangle or a circle will go on forever because there are no rules for proving a mistake: neither side can show there's something wrong with the other person's model as physicists can show there's something wrong with both the wave and particle models. People just go on seeing rectangles and circles till they have the sense to start playing the believing game.

BELIEVING AND DOUBTING AS DIALECTICS

Both games are powerful and important ways of getting to the truth, but they must be played well. By simply using the doubting or the believing muscle, we won't do a very good job of avoiding mistakes. To achieve its potential for getting to the truth, each activity must be worked up into a system with many steps. The doubting muscle's sensitivity to dissonance is not so trustworthy till you work out the rules of logic, transform assertions logically into as many forms as possible, extricate the self, doubt particularly those assertions that seem reasonable, and get opposing propositions to fight each other. Similarly, the believing muscle's ability to project isn't so trustworthy till you build its use into an orderly game and follow the rules: never argue; believe everything, particularly what seems strange or unpleasant; try to put yourself into the skin of people with other perceptions; make metaphorical transformations of assertions to help you enter into them. Most important of all, you must get other people to do it with you, and do it for a long time.

In short, I think both games should be seen as dialectics: testing arenas, market places, laboratories. They are processes which consist of many steps consciously arranged in such a way as to try to be self-correcting and thereby help overcome the natural tendency of the human mind to make mistakes.

The function of a group in the believing game is for people to help each other believe more things, experience more things, and thereby move away from the lowest-common-denominator tendency in a majority conclusion. Suppose, for example, most people in a group find that assertions Number 4 and 5 are the ones they succeed best in believing and hence suspect to be most likely to be true. And they all find it impossible to believe Number 8. But one person there, though he finds he can believe 4 and 5 pretty well, does best with Number 8 and finds the most truth in it. The main process in the believing game is for this person to help the others to have his perception and experience of assertion Number 8. He can tell them more about what he sees, help them to put themselves into it. It may be the best assertion there, but they will only discover it to be so by refraining from arguing and instead trying only to agree or affirm. The existence of a group and the emphasis on investment, projection, and affirmation thus provide a leverage for getting to a truth that is obscure and initially inaccessible, and thereby for avoiding seductive errors.

But the believing game does not have its full power as a dialectic for getting to the truth till you add the dimension of time. After three months of practice, people will be able to understand, believe, and thereby discover obscure truths in assertions which would have been inaccessible to them at the start. Continual practice in trying to have other perceptions and experiences helps people break out of their "sets" and preoccupations—helps them be less rigid, less prey to conventional, knee-jerk, or idiosyncratic responses. It takes practice over time to learn not to "project" in the bad sense—not to see only your own preconceptions or preoccupations; and to learn to "project" more in the good sense—to see more of what's really there by getting more of the self into every bit of it.

I think of the doubting game as the *dialectic of propositions* because the more you get ideas and perceptions into propositional form, the better it works. And I think of the believing game as the *dialectic of experience* because the more you get ideas and perceptions into the most fully experienced form, the better it works.

I would like to compare the way these two dialectics guard against error. To do this, I will specify what I think are the three main sources of human error—the three ways in which man is cognitively "fallen"—and see how both dialectics deal with them.

1. *Self-interest.* It has always been clear that thinking is an act of construction but now psychologists show us more and more how perception too is an act of construction (and that thinking and perception are analogous activities). That is to say, thinking is more like making an estimate in your head than it is like feeding the problem to a computer and getting its answer. Similarly, perception is more like making a drawing than taking a photograph. It is because thinking and perceiving are active and constructional that self-interest has a huge chance to fudge the answer. If we have to add up in our head the three sums of money that are owed to us, we have a good chance to push the answer in the direction we wish. And psychologists have busied themselves for a long time showing how people tend to see what they want to see (that is, draw the picture they want to see instead of being stuck with what shows up on the photograph).

The doubting game or dialectic of propositions tries to attack the problem of self-interest by weeding out the self, its wishes and its preoccupations. It tries to get you to make your thinking more like using a computer than making an estimate in your head. Thus, it sets up a system that is as impersonal as possible: logic, rules for what will pass and what won't, the less involvement of the self the better. It tries to get you to put perceptions or experiences "on paper"—into propostions—and out of your head: do long division rather estimating. Extricate the self, run impersonal transformations. And in addition, it encourages people always to argue with you and assume you are wrong and try to find the holes in your argument that result from your self-interest.

The believing game, on the other hand, is built on the idea that the self cannot be removed: complete objectivity is impossible. Since you can't get away from self-interest, you are given constant practice in trying to get the feel of your own self-interest and to adopt the self-interest of as many other people as possible. Instead of trying to minimize the drawing and estimating models of perception and thinking, the believing game tries to exploit them: you are constantly asked to make the other person's drawing, make the other person's estimate.

2. The second natural human error is *projection:* thinking you see something outside yourself when really it isn't there and you have only "projected" it from inside. If you have food on your mind you are apt to see it everywhere. This happens because perception and thinking are not only acts of construction, they are acts of construction based on previous acts of construction—they are categorizings of new material on the basis of our old categories. We can only see what we already understand and thus we can only see outside our heads things that are already inside our heads. Therefore, there is always a tendency to be wrong about something new: it will tend to be seen either as something familiar or else not seen at all.

The doubting game tries to get away from projection. It is constant practice in trying to look out for mistakes born of projection, constant exercise in trying to remove the self. But the characteristic of mistakes that come from projection is that they don't show up as mistakes unless you can get outside the system and look at it from the vantage point of a completely different model. You can't tell that you are projecting unless you succeed in adopting a different view of what you are looking at—a view which will inevitably seem more wrong at first even though eventually you will realize it is more right.

The believing game is built on the idea that you can't get away from projection since it is the very mechanism for knowing and seeing—and that the culprit is not projection but inflexible and limited projection. Dealing with novelty well doesn't mean emptying the mind of past categories—that just makes for stupidity—but rather getting better at building past categories into new and original arrangements. The believing game is constant practice in getting the mind to see or think what is new, different, alien.

The doubting game emphasizes a model of knowing as an act of discrimination: putting something on trial to see whether it is wanting or not. And it seems to emphasize the camera and template models of perception: testing some input against a model.

The believing game emphasizes a model of knowing as an act of constructing, an act of investment, an act of involvement: what Michael Polanyi calls "the fiduciary transaction."[12] Perception is controlled projection. Ulrich Neisser points out that there is no way to distinguish between believing and hallucinating as processes. Though one is right and the other wrong, both are the same sort of construction out of stimulus-information on the basis of past categories.[13]

3. The human mind also tends to err simply by its lack of precision. It is more like an analogue than a digital computer. Its natural language is "sort of." The doubting game is better than the believing game at correcting for this. It tries to make the mind as much as possible like a computer and constantly tries to check for imprecision and mistakes.

Though the believing game produces less precision, what I

12. *Personal Knowledge,* New York, 1958.
13. *Cognitive Psychology,* New York, 1967, pp. 118ff.

wish to stress here is that it does represent a huge advance in precision over undisciplined thinking. And that using the doubting game in the realm where it doesn't work is nothing but undisciplined thinking.

THE TWO DIALECTICS AS GAMES

It's true that you can't force someone to play the believing game. If he doesn't want to try honestly to believe all assertions, stop arguing, and try to enter into other people's perceptions and experiences, there is nothing you can do to force him. This is too bad, perhaps. But neither can you force someone to accept the rules of logic and play the doubting game. It sometimes seems as though you can but that's only because we have defined the intellectual world as a club where the ticket of admission is a willingness to abide by the rules of the doubting game. The huge numbers of people who are not members of that club—who started out, most of them, as children enjoying the rule-governed process of trying to figure out the truth but somewhere in their lives (usually in school) grew sleepy or angry at the game—these people are a testimony to the fact that you cannot force people to play a game they don't want to play.

Unnecessary attrition from the doubting game is caused by people who play it without realizing it is a game. One of the most important fruits of this whole investigation of the believing game is the heightened realization that the doubting game is *only* a game—and it's *not the only* game.

If you are playing basketball and someone starts carrying the ball around without dribbling or keeping score wrong, what you do next is not part of the game but part of real life. You can shoot him, you can try to have him locked up, you can cry, you can say you won't play with him tomorrow, or you can try to persuade him to start playing again by talking to him. Here, I think the believing game has an inherent advantage over the doubting game. The activity of the believing game (trying to share perceptions and experiences) is more likely than the activity of the doubting game (trying to find holes in the other person's view) to keep people willing to talk to each other if the game breaks down.

I am not arguing against rules but *for* rules. The power and fun of a game is in the submission to a set of rules. The pleasure of a game is in the ritualized process itself, its coherence and structure, rather than in a final goal or content. The release of energy and spirits characteristic of a game also comes from this submission to rules and structure: because one is in a rule-bound structure—because it is not real life—one can let down some of one's guard, and there is a sense of release.

Both games are probably inherently social. Language and reasoning are probably simulations in a single mind of processes first occurring between minds. Socrates thought of reasoning as necessarily a social process. I think that is part of the reason he refused to write anything down. And the doubting game still benefits from being played by a group rather than as solitaire. But because we have taken it for granted so long and worked at it so much, we tend to be much better at it when alone than we are at the believing game. When we are more practiced at the believing game, more people will be better at playing it alone. But I suspect it will remain more inherently social since it is *only* a group which gives the believing game its maximum trustworthiness.

For entrance into the intellectual world, we tend to require willingness to play the doubting game. This would be all right if we also required willingness to play the believing game and said to people who refuse to play, as we say to people who refuse to play the doubting game: "What a foolish, irrational, and self-indulgent person you are. You must be trying to preserve some favorite self-delusion as a security blanket."

We can see, then, something about how to apply all this to the reality of school and college activity. Though the two games are complementary and mutually beneficial, they cannot be played simultaneously. We cannot say, "Well let's try not only to be as critical as we can, but also be a bit more believing too." Though that's really what we want in the end, when adopted as an immediate goal it results in mere muddling: people merely doubting what's easy to doubt but never questioning what they don't want to question; and at the same time believing what's easy to believe and never risking swallowing what is alien. Each should be played in severely delimited ways: presented as artificial activities of heightened organization, structure, and energy expenditure. With a definite end so you can stop and rest. One or two hours a week in which people really played the believing game well—that is, really followed the rules—and another hour or two in which they really played the doubting game well: that would be a revolution.

THE BELIEVING GAME IN ACTION:
FIGHTING THE ITCH FOR CLOSURE

The teacherless class is a perfect laboratory for playing the believing game. But I would also hope to see it in school, college, and intellectual activities in general. Toward this end, a special note is necessary about closure.

I advocate the believing game not just because it is nice or sociable, not even just because the doubting game doesn't work everywhere, but because the believing game yields the truth. It is a way of coming up with right answers. Yet one of the things that must be stressed most as advice for playing the believing game is that you must learn to inhibit your impulse for answers.

For one thing, any group which starts playing the believing game cannot usually produce answers worth any trust in less than a couple of months or more. The process is a long, slow discipline involving growth and increased flexibility.

But also, trying for an answer is what leads most often to argu-

ments, defensiveness, and possessiveness ("Did *my* idea or perception turn out to be the right answer?"). The itch for closure
brings the itch for argument. Playing the believing game means
fighting the itch for closure.

In playing, therefore, decide hardheadedly what kind of truth
you need and how soon you need it. You'll find that if you answer
honestly, you'll need much less than you are in the habit of trying for.

What kind of truth do you need? There is a dirtier and a
cleaner truth, and the believing game settles, much of the time,
for the dirtier kind: truth mixed with error. Many people would
say you haven't got the truth unless you have it free from error:
part of our feeling for the word "truth" is certainty. But this feeling misleads us. If you have three answers and one of them is
true, you *have* the truth—even if you don't know which one it is.
This may sound like sophistry but it's not: 1. If you don't settle
for this dirty mixture, you might not *get* that truth at all: if you
are too fastidious and try to force assertions always to prove themselves at the door, you lose some of your best and most accurate
perceptions (and those of other people working with you). 2. You
can *benefit* from the truth in this mixed dirty bag: if you look at,
ponder, and digest all three answers—even if you still don't know
which is right—you will learn from the right one. Your organism
can do a lot of sifting that you cannot do consciously. Like the
owl eating the mouse.

How soon do you need your truth? Many activities that could
be called intellectual—especially most school activities—fulfill their
goals perfectly if they slow down on generating final answers but
speed up the business of making people more perceptive and intelligent. The shape of the believing game is waiting, patience,
not being in a hurry. Answers come later: finally comes a reorientation of thinking or perception that makes clear the answer to an
issue that was raised much earlier. Now it is clear without argument or uncertainty: earlier you would have had to argue for an

answer and you might well have gotten the wrong one (along
with unnecessary commitments to various answers on the part of
the arguers). Waiting brings naturally a shared, accurate perception—closure. Week by week you improve the quality of the pool
of perceptions and assertions you *refrain* from choosing among.

So if you are playing the believing game and you need answers
at the end of three months, spend the first 2½ months not-trying
for them. If you only have an hour, spend the first 50 minutes
not-looking for answers.

It helps in all this to be more conscious of the itch for closure.
Notice how most of us have a habit of trying to achieve closure—
settlement of at least *something*—by the end of any class or meeting. Even at the end of a 30-minute enterprise of any sort, we
want to say, "Well, now, let's see what we've settled." Try to feel
how stupid this impulse is—how the desire for closure impedes
any larger slower reorderings of thought or experience and really
serves the mind's desire to stay the same.

THE TWO GAMES AS REINFORCERS
OF DIFFERENT CHARACTER TRAITS

I find associated with each dialectic a whole set of character traits
—both cognitive and affective. Each set makes a kind of interrelated net or complex of styles:

Doubting Game	Believing Game
extrication, disengagement	involvement
detachment, perspective	projection, commitment
rejecting or fending off what is new	willingness to explore what is new
closing, clenching	opening, loosening
literal	metaphorical

rigid	flexible
stubborn, hanging on	yielding
impulse for security	impulse for risk
centered, unmoving self	floating self
learning to be sharper, finer, more piercing, harder, tougher	learning to be larger, more encompassing, softer, more absorbent
aggressive: meeting threat by beating it down	nonaggressive: meeting threat by bending, incorporating; nonviolent
deflating	supporting
competitive	cooperative
solitary or adversary activity	working in a group
talking, noise, arguing	listening, silence, agreeing

Clearly I see great values in the qualities down the right side of the page. But I am not really knocking the ones on the left: they are necessary and valuable as long as they are balanced by their complements. But only the left side is reinforced by our culture's conception of intellectuality. I would like to sum up this psychological contrast by pointing to three other ways of viewing it.

1. There is a contrast here between the thirst for certainty and an acceptance of uncertainty and ambiguity. The doubting game represents such a thirst for certainty that it tends to confuse *certainty* with *truth*. This confusion is so widespread that many people equate the two. Yet they are fully distinct. Whether a proposition is certain or whether it is true are very different matters. Your behavior and the results of your inquiries are likely to be very different according to how greatly you insist on certainty.

Iago's work is almost done once he gets Othello to the point of needing certainty: only one answer is acceptable—infidelity. Fidelity is incapable of being determined with certainty. The need for certainty, then, tends to carry in itself a drift toward certain kinds

of investigations and certain kinds of results. There are some
kinds of data and propositions and insights a person cannot benefit from if he has no tolerance for working with uncertainty.

2. There is also a contrast here between male and female as our
culture defines them. The monopoly of the doubting game tends
to reinforce those personal styles which the culture also defines as
male: aggressive, thrusting, combative, competitive, and initiatory. A woman tends to be perceived as less feminine if she shines
in the doubting game—if she loves to initiate and win arguments
and find holes in the other person's position. A man tends to be
perceived as less masculine if his intellectual style is *not* that of
the doubting game—if he operates by pliancy, absorbency, non-
initiation, and nonaggression. Some of our language for the adversary process of the doubting game reveals these associations of
gender: "advancing points," "making points," "seeing if a point
stands up," "finding holes," and "poking holes" in the other person's argument. Both the culture in general and the intellectual community in particular suffer a loss of power from this
onesidedness.

3. There is also a contrast between two different qualities of
energy. The doubting game—the adversary method—involves a
combative kind of energy that feels like clenching a muscle: sending current to a muscle to make it contract. Words like "tight"
and "hard" characterize the energy in a good argument. There is
an initiatory and cutting quality. A good arguer really cuts—cuts
through issues, through fog, through excess fat—pierces to the
center of things.

The energy that goes with the believing game—especially in
trying to *begin* to play—is that peculiar, delicate energy required
to keep something energetically open. It is like the energy you
send—whatever the physiology is—to keep a muscle from contract-
ing. Perhaps it is like muscle *tonus:* though the muscle is not sag-
ging or limp, neither is it tight or rigid. To *try* to put out this
kind of energy is difficult because "trying" seems to make you

contract muscles. Trying to remain *open* is a kind of trying-to-not-try. A room full of people having an argument produces a high energy level. But if you ask them to stop arguing and to agree with each other's assertions, the energy level is very apt to go way down and most of them will feel you've asked them to do something sleepy and boring. Intellectuals in particular often feel that if they cannot argue and try to cut through error, the only other thing they can do is just go soft and limp.

The energy that occurs when people are *successful* in playing the believing game is easier to describe: it is the release of energy that comes from the "ah-ha" experience of reorientation or gestalt-shift. When you succeed in seeing something the way someone else sees it—and it is different from the way you have been seeing it—this almost invariably produces a little burst or release of energy in you. There are experiments showing that when children "get" something—at the moment of reorientation or "ah-ha" —they almost invariably display a sudden little physical movement or release of tension.[14]

FEARS OF THE BELIEVING GAME

Before the believing game can be fully legitimized, a whole set of fears must be spoken to. There is a natural feeling that the doubting game guards against various kinds of loose or self-indulgent thinking which undermine truthseeking. To legitimize the believing game would seem to invite, for example, solipsism, groupthink, and credulity.

Solipsism. It might seem at first that the believing game would invite people to tune out all thoughts and perceptions except their own. For the believing game keeps other people from arguing with you. But this is only to promote the main process: get-

14 Gertrude Hendrix, "A New Clue to Transfer of Training," *Elementary School Journal*, Dec. 1947, pp. 198-200; cited in Morris L. Bigge, *Learning Theory for Teachers* (New York, 1964), p. 283.

ting you continually to move out of your own perceptions and thoughts into someone else's. The believing game is a tool for *breaking out of* solipsism.

Surprisingly enough, it is the doubting game which, in our culture at least, is the main encourager of solipsism. It is very common for intellectuals and academics—though they lack the traditional, heavy-lidded mannerisms of the solipsist—actually to use argument and dialectic to defend themselves against ever having the perception, experience, and thought of other people. Such abusers of the doubting game allow themselves to stay locked into their own minds because they feel it is legitimate never genuinely to entertain a different view if they can mount a strong attack against it.

Groupthink. Like solipsism, this is a serious pathology for a truthseeking community. And again it seems as though the doubting game would be the best defense against it: the goal of the doubting game is disproof, and disproof is how the wise individual or minority changes the mind of the erroneous majority. The trouble is that disproof is possible in only a relatively small proportion of important questions. Otherwise, you can argue against someone till the cows come home, you can say you have "disproved" or "demolished" or "shattered" or "found gaping holes in" his position. But he is very liable to be unpersuaded because in fact you have *not* disproven his case. How much harder to persuade not just an individual but a majority with a sense of orthodoxy and authority on its side. The doubting game then *supports* groupthink because it promotes the feeling that a new or minority idea must disprove the reigning one before it need be seriously entertained—which in most cases is not possible.

The believing game gives the little man much more power over the majority than the doubting game does. It is the essence of the believing game that the majority spends all its time not merely not-arguing against the individual, not merely listening to him, but actually trying to believe him.

Credulity. The problem of credulity looks like the problem of insufficient "critical thinking." Critical thinking is what is supposed to prevent people from believing what credulous people believe. When people write material for college catalogues or try to justify certain studies, they often speak of teaching critical thinking. I don't want to deny the value of critical thinking any more than I would deny the value of the doubting game.

But there's another way of looking at credulity or the problem of people believing things they shouldn't believe. When we call someone credulous we usually mean *not* that he believes X because he has never heard of Y, but that he has heard of both X and Y and believes X when he shouldn't. The productive question is *why* does he believe X. The reason is usually one of the following: X was told him by an authority such as his parents or his teacher or his government; X is something that is in fashion; X is something he worked out himself; X is a view that is crucial to his very conception of himself or his reality; or X is an instance of a *kind* of thinking he is particularly open to believing—it fits the structure of his thinking—(for example, magical thinking or scientific thinking). Other reasons could be listed, but they could all be summed up by saying that for him X *was easier to believe than Y*. All humans have a propensity to believe what is easy to believe rather than what is true. We call credulous those who do this most.

This diagnosis would be fine if only we didn't turn around and give the disease the wrong name. The "credulous" person really suffers from *difficulty* in believing, not ease in believing: give him an array of assertions and he will always believe the one that requires the least expenditure of believing energy. He has a weak believing muscle and can only believe what is easy to believe. He can only digest what has been prechewed. The fact that we call this disease credulity when it is really incredulity reflects vividly our culture's fear of belief.

Behind the problems of solipsism, groupthink, and (in)credulity—which are indeed pathologies in a community of truthseekers —lies, I think, one single problem: the inability to change your mind. The main hindrance to the search for truth is probably the inability to abandon a present belief and adopt a better one when it comes along—even though it may be harder to believe, or may involve admitting you were wrong, or may come from someone you don't want to agree with.

An analysis of mind-changing is in order. I use myself as an example. I admit I am stubborn and love to argue. But I think that makes me typical of intellectuals and academics.

Sometimes the doubting game works just the way it's supposed to: I believe something I shouldn't; someone argues against it; this serves as a booster shot of critical thinking, I realize I shouldn't have believed it, and I stop. But actually it seldom works so nicely—for me or for others.

In many cases the doubting game has the opposite effect: I experience it as a strong attack and I dig in my heels the harder.

In many other cases, it *looks* as though the doubting game worked. It looks as though I was blasted out of my bad position. But not really. I went through the motions, admitted I was wrong, thought I had changed my mind, but deep down I retained my primary allegiance to my first love, the ostensibly abandoned idea. A close look at my behavior and the implications of my speech shows that I still operate on the basis of the error.

And then there are the cases—no doubt far too few—where I actually *did* change my mind. But what strikes me is that it was not, in fact, the process of being devastatingly argued against that did it. Or at least that wasn't sufficient. Whenever I really changed my mind, there was always a something else that had to happen before I would stop fighting, admit error, and in fact really change my mind—instead of just going through the motions. That something else is a bit mysterious, but I can say something about when it happens most and what it feels like. It happens most when the person arguing against me lets up on his guns a little, stops trying to show that I'm an idiot, and in fact shows some glimmer of understanding for why *I* believe what I do believe. He shows a bit of willingness to share *my* perception: then I'm more willing to share his. And subjectively there is a very definite feel for this thing which permits a change of mind: it feels like a letting go, a relinquishing, a giving up of a piece of stubbornness. Even, in a sense, a giving up of a piece of myself. Saying goodbye to a love affair I wish weren't finished.

The believing game helps this mind-changing process more than the doubting game does. Though the believing game is in-taking or incorporatory, nevertheless this taking-in permits a greater letting-go. The doubting game, on the other hand, rein-forces hanging on. Defending something against all attacks re-wards the universal tendency to hang on at all costs to what you have. Letting-go requires an atmosphere of acceptance and trust, and the believing game helps inspire this atmosphere much more than the doubting game does.

I believe that people in the academic and intellectual world (especially in the humanities and social sciences) suffer badly from a characteristic inability to change their minds. I attribute this problem to an excessive reliance upon the doubting game. It is my sense that the more people shine at the doubting game, the more they tend to be stubborn and unwilling to change their minds.

There are more personal emotional fears that reinforce the mo-nopoly of the doubting game and which must therefore be ex-plored here. I think we all fear, to a greater or lesser extent, being taken over, infected, or controlled by a bad or wrong idea. The believing game asks us, as it were, to sleep with any idea that comes down the road. To be promiscuous. We will turn into the girl who just can't say no. A yes-man. A flunky. A slave. Someone who can be made to believe anything. A large opening that any-thing can be poured into. Force-fed. Raped.

Everyone feels his self is fragile in some way. At the psychic level I think the main function of the doubting game is to guard against such indiscriminate invasion of the self. We naturally feel we are liable to poisoning or infection by what is alien. Often enough in life we must submit to *contact* with such material, but actually taking it inside is too much. And we *can* avoid that. Descartes, the archetypal player of the doubting game when he doubted everything and then only readmitted clear and distinct ideas, was among other things engaging in a purification rite. He was reenacting the parable of sweeping the house clean of evil spirits with a new broom. A common use of the doubting game in intellectual discourse is a version of the same thing: no idea is truly listened to, truly taken in, unless it has been "purified" by the ritual of the doubting game.

What is finally becoming clear, I think, through increased understanding of human emotional and cognitive functioning, is that you can *never* produce enough security clearance, no matter how new or powerful your broom: you can *never* keep out all wrong ideas, all disgusting or threatening ideas, all ideas tainted by previous tenants—all infection. The only cure for this problem is metaphorically specified in Conrad's phrase in *Lord Jim:* "In the destructive element immerse." Since you can't keep ideas out, you have to let them in: consider things in the guise of the widest and most conflicting array of categories and thereby get a feel for what's really there—a feel for the misconceptions or blindings that various categories impose on us.[15]

There is a kind of validity to this fear. The sense of fragility of self—the need for integrity of one's borders—is no joke. You cannot and probably should not ask people to immerse themselves in ideas that are too much for them. But also, correspondingly, you shouldn't trust someone's judgment who is too touchy in his fear of invasion. What is needed is practice in learning to im-

[15] This is the thesis of an important book by Colin Turbayne, *The Myth of Metaphor*, University of South Carolina Press, 1970.

merse the self *gradually* in the element perceived as dangerous—
and it is just such a process that is constituted by the believing
game.

SPECULATIONS ON THE HISTORY
OF THE BELIEVING GAME

There are probably historical reasons why the doubting game has
been monopolistic and tried to deny legitimacy to the believing
game. In the past the tables were probably turned: people probably once used a kind of believing game and didn't use a doubting game at all. It is easier and more natural to use the believing
muscle and put oneself into an assertion than it is to use the
doubting muscle and extricate oneself from it and assume it is
false. It's in the very nature of perceiving and thinking to project,
enter in, or participate. It was probably only through great
struggle over many centuries of intellectual development that men
learned to do this artificial, paradoxical, and powerful thing of
perceiving and understanding something but at the same time trying to assume it is false in order to make errors turn up. Doubting
something is like doing two contrary things at the same time:
having an idea and *rejecting* it. In many languages, the word
"doubt" is cognate with the word for "two" ("double"): being "of
two minds." So although we're in trouble now from a weakness in
believing, no doubt we used to get into trouble from a weakness
in doubting.

  In fact, the fully developed believing game as I conceive it—a
fully developed system with many steps—wasn't possible till the
development of the doubting game. We only learned from the
doubting game how to turn the exercise of a muscle into a full
dialectic—how to turn thought into something more than sitting
down and clenching your jaw and furrowing your brow as hard
as you can. The development of the doubting game—logical dia-

lectic—was the development for the first time of an artificial, systematic, many-step process in which the very artificiality of it acts as a corrective to what you would have "just thought"—no matter how smart you were. Now we know how to make the believing game into this kind of dialectic. But I think the believing game has been developing and trying to be born for a long time and it is interesting to note past forms.

1. The most recent—and one which has influenced me—is the development of group process. Therapy groups and encounter groups often operate by principles similar to what I describe for the believing game. Often there is a ground rule that instead of trying to prove assertions wrong, it is more helpful to get them into the form of statements of perception and experience such that other people can try to share them.

2. Quaker meetings in which no decisions are taken except by consensus. This seems a full and precise use of the believing game. Obviously Quaker meetings are not based on a denial of disagreement. (Indeed Quakers are particularly strong disagreers or scruplers: they have particularly strong doubting muscles or sensitivities to dissonance. It may be that Quakers developed their consensus process because they were way ahead of the rest of us in arguing and disagreeing.)

   A meeting in the Quaker manner is an explicit *refusal* to settle for the lowest common denominator—a refusal to settle on that decision which invites the fewest arguments or objections: there is always at least one serious objection and one is too many. Rather it insists on achieving that decision the entire group can best *enter into* or *affirm*. In short, it is not a matter of "which course of action do we doubt least" but rather "which course of action can we all believe most."

3. Juries. The court of law is above all an adversary arena, a playing of the doubting game, a contest for finding holes in the other fellow's argument. But if there is only the doubting game,

why the jury? Lawyers and judges are far better at doubting and finding inconsistencies, whether in assertions of fact or of law. To bring in a jury is to bring in people who are *least* qualified to play the doubting game. What's more, not only are they specifically barred from doubting game processes, they are also forced into believing game processes: they may not talk or ask questions of witnesses, lawyers, nor scarcely of the judge; they may only sit in silence and listen. Listening and silence are hallmarks of the believing game. All input, no output. And until a recent Supreme Court decision which seems contrary to the tradition, juries had to arrive at unanimous decisions. Thus, like a Quaker meeting, though members may doubt all they want, the process by which they can best fulfill their task is the process of concerted affirmation.

Obviously juries and Quaker-run meetings *permit* situations in which people exhaustedly settle for a decision that no one likes but it was the only one which no one hates. But when this happens, you can feel that something has gone wrong. You can feel the structure was trying to foster the opposite process: a more positive dialectic which gets people out of their partisan point of view, out of their initial way of thinking, and thus helps them to grow and change. Consensus can usually happen only when something organic occurs in a group. Even the co-ercive, tension-producing and exhaustion-producing element in this sort of meeting—"no one may go home till there is consensus!"—helps people break out of "sets" or habitual points of view: this is the essential process in the believing game.

4. People like Thomas Kuhn and Michael Polanyi (*op. cit.*) give an account of the history of science to the effect that though scientists almost universally feel they practice the doubting game, nevertheless important cruxes are settled by something very like the believing game. (Though only big wheels get to play.) At a period of scientific revolution—when competing paradigms or models are up for grabs—it is as it is with read-

ings of a poem: the "wrong" paradigm is not proven wrong; rather those who carry weight in the profession perceive another one as more fruitful and indeed truer. They perceive this truth from within it, not from without.

5. I have earlier tried to show that when literary critics really do their business well, they are playing the believing game.

CONCLUSION: THE INTERDEPENDENCE
OF THE TWO GAMES

My case for the believing game can be summed up in two assertions.

1. It is the only process for getting to the truth in areas of word-interpretation and gestalt-making. 2. It is a disciplined intellectual dialectic whose practice makes people more perceptive, flexible, and generally more intelligent; and it reinforces character traits which our culture badly needs.

In much of my thinking about this matter I have seen the doubting game as villain. I think bad things can be associated with the doubting game: by helping people extricate themselves from perception, it can reinforce self-deception; by helping people extricate themselves from experience, it can reinforce the peculiarly antiseptic inhumanity that is characteristic of our culture, and make it easier, for instance, to drop bombs on people.

But previous drafts showed me that the doubting game is not in itself the villain. (And also showed me the depth of my own commitment to the doubting game.) For the ability to extricate oneself from ideas, to reduce experiences to propositions, to transform propositions logically, to achieve detachment, to cut through crap, to be combative and thrusting, to be fiercely stubborn, to have a hunger for certainty, to doubt everything, to have a dug-in and unmoving self—all these qualities are extremely valuable. People rarely achieve anything good without them.

The two games are interdependent. I can close by saying that the believing game needs to be legitimized if only for the sake of the doubting game. For one thing, there is a growing movement of revulsion against the doubting game which will subside only when the believing game has equal legitimacy. For another thing, along with playing the doubting game too much, people play it shoddily, and they will considerably improve when they start playing the believing game too. We learn to play the doubting game "in general"—not realizing it is a game. What that means is that we learn critical thinking "in general"—that is, we learn, as it were, to try in general to be more vigilant, try in general to doubt everything, try in general not to be a sucker. But we don't apply this practice to everything. When it comes to really important things, people don't really doubt them. "After all," we say to ourselves unconsciously, "you've got to believe *something*." But that's wrong. It shows we don't understand the doubting game. You don't have to believe *anything*: it's only a game and for the game you must doubt absolutely everything and see what you come up with.

In short, the two games are only halves of a full cycle of thinking. Because human functioning is organic and developmental, because for example you cannot learn to be a cut-throat editor till you learn to be a prolific producer, so too people cannot learn to play well either the doubting game or the believing game till they also learn to play the other one well.

A Few Books to Help with Correct Usage

CORRECT usage and good writing are not the same. Both are good things but it helps not to confuse them. In the writing class, concentrate on making your writing work better. Correct usage is a simpler matter that you can get by yourself out of books.

For looking up something you are not sure of, here are a few books I have found useful:

THE AMERICAN HERITAGE DICTIONARY OF THE ENGLISH LANGUAGE, Houghton Mifflin Co., Education Division, 110 Tremont St., Boston, Mass. 02107

REFERENCE MANUAL FOR STENOGRAPHERS AND TYPISTS, Gavin and Sabin, McGraw-Hill Book Co., 1221 Avenue of the Americas, New York, N.Y. 10020. (I find this book particularly useful because it doesn't try to teach me things I don't want to know, it just gives me the answer I'm looking for in the quickest way possible.)

WRITER'S GUIDE AND INDEX TO ENGLISH, Porter Perrin et al., Scott, Foresman and Co., 1900 E. Lake Ave., Glenview, Ill. 60025

For learning spelling, usage, and grammar, here are some programmed books that you can use entirely on your own:

SPELLING IMPROVEMENT: A PROGRAM FOR SELF-INSTRUCTION, Patricia Fergus, McGraw-Hill (see address above).

BASIC SPELLING SKILLS: A PROGRAM FOR SELF-INSTRUCTION, Learning Technology, Inc., McGraw-Hill (see address above).

PROGRAMED REVIEW OF ENGLISH, UNIT I, SPELLING, Martha S. Trimble, Harper and Row, Inc., Scranton, Pa. 18512

UNIT II, DICTION

UNIT III, WRITING

ENGLISH # 3200: A PROGRAMED COURSE IN GRAMMAR AND USAGE, Joseph C. Blumenthal, Harcourt Brace Jovanovich, Inc., 757 Third Ave., New York, N.Y. 10017. This seems to be the most widely used of the programmed texts.)

COMPETENCE IN ENGLISH: A PROGRAMED HANDBOOK, J. H. Hook and R. L. Stevens, Harcourt Brace Jovanovich (see address above).

NECESSARY INGREDIENTS:

Get a commitment from at least seven people for a ten-week stretch

Make sure everyone writes something every week

Make sure everything read out loud is read twice and given a minute's silence after each reading

Give *pointing* and *summarizing* responses to every piece of writing

Make sure everyone, for his first four classes, uses two showing exercises

Do three ten-minute writing exercises each week

Use the last five minutes of each class for reactions to the class itself

GIVING MOVIES OF YOUR MIND:

Pointing (p. 85)

Summarizing (p. 86)

Telling (p. 87)

Showing (p. 70: voices; motion, locomotion; weather: clothing; terrain; colors; shapes; animals; vegetables; musical instruments; body; where it's evolved from, where evolving to; writer's real intention, crazy intention; what it was written instead of; what the writer did before writing it; portrait of anonymous writer; writing as clay; reactions of someone else; picture or doodle; sounds; jabbering; movements; ten-minute writing; meditation)

FURTHER ADVICE TO READERS:
Make sure you've had a good chance to read the writing (p. 93)
One reader at a time, or all at once? (p. 93)
Never quarrel with someone else's reaction (p. 94)
Give specific reactions to specific parts (p. 94)
No kind of reaction is wrong (p. 95: "content" as opposed to
    "style"; odd reactions; advice; evaluation; theories; irrelevant
    reactions)
Though no reactions are wrong, you still have to try to read well
    (p. 98)
Sometimes you may not want to (p. 99)
You are always right and always wrong (p. 100)

ADVICE TO THE WRITER ON LISTENING:
Be quiet and listen (p. 101)
Don't try to understand what people tell you (p. 102)
But do try to understand *how* they tell it to you (p. 102)
Don't reject what readers tell you (p. 102)
Don't stop them from giving you reactions (p. 104)
But don't be tyrannized by what they say (p. 104)
Ask for what you want but don't play teacher with them (p. 105)
You are always right and always wrong (p. 106)